Conference of the North American Chapter of the Association for Computational Linguistics: Human Language Technologies (NAACL HLT 2022)

Tutorial Abstracts

Online
10 - 15 July 2022

ISBN: 978-1-7138-5622-1

Printed from e-media with permission by:

Curran Associates, Inc.
57 Morehouse Lane
Red Hook, NY 12571

proceedings.com

Some format issues inherent in the e-media version may also appear in this print version.

Association for Computational Linguistics
209 N. Eighth Street
Stroudsburg, Pennsylvania 18360

Phone: 1-570-476-8006
Fax: 1-570-476-0860

acl@aclweb.org

Additional copies of this publication are available from:

Curran Associates, Inc.
57 Morehouse Lane
Red Hook, NY 12571 USA
Phone: 845-758-0400
Fax: 845-758-2633
Email: curran@proceedings.com
Web: www.proceedings.com

NAACL 2022

The 2022 Conference of the North American Chapter of the Association for Computational Linguistics: Human Language Technologies

Tutorial Abstracts

July 10-15, 2022

Order copies of this and other ACL proceedings from:

Association for Computational Linguistics (ACL)
209 N. Eighth Street
Stroudsburg, PA 18360
USA
Tel: +1-570-476-8006
Fax: +1-570-476-0860
acl@aclweb.org

Introduction

Welcome to the Tutorials Session of NAACL 2022!

The tutorials give an opportunity to the NAACL conference attendees to be lectured by highly qualified expert researchers on cutting-edge and new relevant upcoming topics in our research community.

As in previous years, the organization (including submission, reviewing and selection) were coordinated jointly with other conferences in the 2022 calendar year: ACL, NAACL, COLING and EMNLP. We formed a review committee of 34 members, which includes the NAACL tutorial chairs, the ACL tutorial chairs, the COLING tutorial chairs, the EMNLP tutorial chairs and 23 external reviewers (see Program Committee for the full list). We organized a reviewing process so that each proposal received at least 3 reviews. Tutorials were evaluated based on their clarity, novelty, timely character of the topic, diversity and inclusion, instructor's experience, likely audience interest and open access of the tutorial instructional material. We received a total of 47 tutorial submissions, of which 6 were selected for presentation at NAACL, considering the preferences expressed by authors and the relevance for the NAACL research community.

We solicited two types of tutorials, namely cutting-edge themes and introductory themes. The 6 tutorials for NAACL include one introductory tutorial and five cutting-edge tutorials. The introductory tutorial is dedicated to Human-Centered Evaluation of Explanations (T4). The cutting-edge tutorials are: (T1) Text Generation with Text-Editing Models, (T2) Self-supervised Representation Learning for Speech Processing, (T3) New Frontiers of Information Extraction, (T5) Multimodal Machine Learning, and (T6) Contrastive Data and Learning for Natural Language Processing. NAACL 2022 tutorials are delivered in a live hybrid format and also available as pre-recorded captioned videos, with additional live Q&A sessions.

We would like to thank the tutorial authors for their quick responses and flexibility while organizing the conference in a hybrid mode. We are also grateful to the 23 external reviewers for their invaluable help in the decision process. Finally, we thank the conference organizers for effective collaboration, the general chair Dan Roth, the program chairs (Marine Carpuat, Marie-Catherine de Marneffe and Ivan Vladimir Meza Ruiz), the publication chair Ryan Cotterell, and the authors of `aclpub2` with special mention to Jordan Zhang and Danilo Croce.

NAACL 2022 Tutorial Co-chairs,

Miguel Ballesteros
Yulia Tsvetkov
Cecilia O. Alm

Organizing Committee

General Chair

Dan Roth, University of Pennsylvania & AWS AI Labs, USA

Program Chairs

Marine Carpuat, University of Maryland, USA
Marie-Catherine de Marneffe de Marneffe, Ohio State University, USA
Ivan Vladimir Meza Ruiz, National Autonomous University of Mexico, Mexico

Tutorial Chairs

Miguel Ballesteros, AWS AI Labs, USA
Yulia Tsvetkov, University of Washington, USA
Cecilia O. Alm, Rochester Institute of Technology, USA

Program Committee

Program Committee

Cecilia O. Alm, Rochester Institute of Technology, USA
Antonios Anastasopoulos, George Mason University, USA
Miguel Ballesteros, AWS AI Labs, USA
Daniel Beck, University of Melbourne, Australia
Luciana Benotti, National University of Córdoba, Argentina
Yevgeni Berzak, Technion, Israel Institute of Technology, Israel
Erik Cambria, Nanyang Technological University, Singapore
Hsin-Hsi Chen, National Taiwan University, Taiwan
Gaël Dias, University of Caen Normandy, France
Lucia Donatelli, Saarland University, Germany
Samhaa R. El-Beltagy, Newgiza University, Egypt
Karën Fort, Sorbonne Université / LORIA, France
Heng Ji, University of Illinois, Urbana-Champaign, USA
David Jurgens, University of Michigan, USA
Naoaki Okazaki, Tokyo Institute of Technology, Japan
Alexis Palmer, University of Colorado, Boulder, USA
Mohammad Taher Pilehvar, Tehran Institute for Advanced Studies, Iran
Barbara Plank, LMU Munich, Germany and IT University of Copenhagen, Denmark
Emily Prud'hommeaux, Boston College, USA
Xipeng Qiu, Fudan University, China
Agata Savary, Université Paris-Saclay, France
João Sedoc, New York University, USA
Yulia Tsvetkov, University of Washington, USA
Aline Villavicencio, University of Sheffield, UK
Ivan Vulić, University of Cambridge, UK
Yogarshi Vyas, AWS AI Labs, USA
Joachim Wagner, Dublin City University, Ireland
Taro Watanabe, Nara Institute of Science and Technology, Japan
Aaron Steven White, University of Rochester, USA
Diyi Yang, Georgia Institute of Technology, USA
Marcos Zampieri, Rochester Institute of Technology, USA
Meishan Zhang, Harbin Institute of Technology (Shenzhen), China
Yue Zhang, Westlake University, China
Arkaitz Zubiaga, Queen Mary University London, UK

Table of Contents

Text Generation with Text-Editing Models

Eric Malmi♢, Yue Dong♣, Jonathan Mallinson♢, Aleksandr Chuklin♢, Jakub Adamek♢, Daniil Mirylenka♢, Felix Stahlberg♢, Sebastian Krause♢, Shankar Kumar♢, Aliaksei Severyn♢

♢Google

♣McGill University & Mila

text-editing-tutorial@google.com

Abstract

Text-editing models have recently become a prominent alternative to seq2seq models for monolingual text-generation tasks such as grammatical error correction, simplification, and style transfer. These tasks share a common trait – they exhibit a large amount of textual overlap between the source and target texts. Text-editing models take advantage of this observation and learn to generate the output by predicting edit operations applied to the source sequence. In contrast, seq2seq models generate outputs word-by-word from scratch thus making them slow at inference time. Text-editing models provide several benefits over seq2seq models including faster inference speed, higher sample efficiency, and better control and interpretability of the outputs. This tutorial[1] provides a comprehensive overview of text-editing models and current state-of-the-art approaches, and analyzes their pros and cons. We discuss challenges related to productionization and how these models can be used to mitigate hallucination and bias, both pressing challenges in the field of text generation.

1 Introduction

After revolutionizing the field of machine translation (Sutskever et al., 2014; Cho et al., 2014; Bahdanau et al., 2015), sequence-to-sequence (seq2seq) methods have quickly become the standard approach for not only multilingual but also for *monolingual* sequence transduction / text generation tasks, such as text summarization, style transfer, and grammatical error correction. While delivering significant quality gains, these models, however, are prone to hallucinations (Maynez et al., 2020; Pagnoni et al., 2021). The seq2seq task setup (where targets are generated from scratch word by word) overlooks the fact that in many monolingual tasks the source and target sequences have a considerable overlap, hence targets could be reconstructed from the source inputs by applying a set of edit operations.

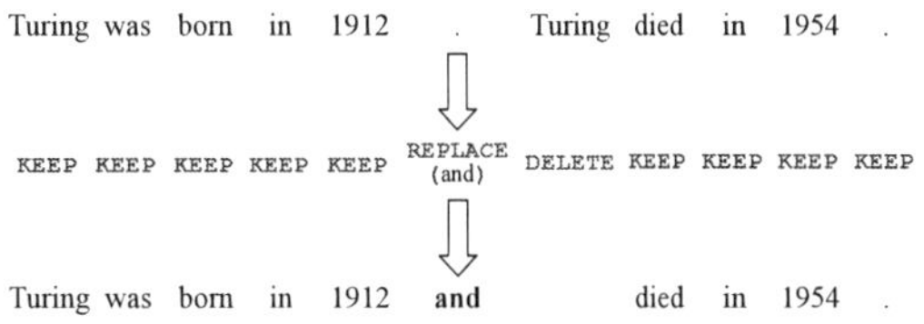

Figure 1: An example of using a text-editing approach to solve a sentence-fusion task.

Text-editing models attempt to address some of the limitations of seq2seq approaches and there has been recently a surge of interest in applying them to a variety of monolingual tasks including text simplification (Dong et al., 2019; Mallinson et al., 2020; Agrawal et al., 2021), grammatical error correction (Awasthi et al., 2019; Omelianchuk et al., 2020; Malmi et al., 2019; Stahlberg and Kumar, 2020; Rothe et al., 2021; Chen et al., 2020; Hinson et al., 2020; Gao et al., 2021), sentence fusion (Malmi et al., 2019; Mallinson et al., 2020) (see an example in Figure 1), MT automatic post-editing (Gu et al., 2019; Zietkiewicz, 2020; Mallinson et al., 2020), text style transfer (Reid and Zhong, 2021; Malmi et al., 2020), data-to-text generation (Kasner and Dušek, 2020), and utterance rewriting (Liu et al., 2020; Voskarides et al., 2020; Jin et al., 2022).

Text-editing approaches claim to be more accurate or on-par with seq2seq baselines especially in low resource settings, less prone to hallucinations and faster at inference time. These advantages have generated a substantial and continued level of interest in text-editing research. The goal of this tutorial is to provide the first comprehensive overview of the family of text-editing approaches and to offer practical guidelines for applying them to a variety of text-generation tasks.

[1]Website: https://text-editing.github.io/

Proceedings of the 2022 Conference of the North American Chapter of the Association for Computational Linguistics Human Language Technologies: Tutorial Abstracts, pages 1 - 7
July 10-15, 2022 ©2022 Association for Computational Linguistics

Section	Duration
Introduction	15 min
What are text-editing models?	
Text-editing vs. seq2seq models	
Model design	40 min
Example model + model landscape	
Edit-operation types	
Tagging architecture	
Auto-regressiveness	
Converting target texts to target edits	
Applications	45 min
Overview	
Grammatical Error Correction	
Text Simplification	
Unsupervised Style Transfer	
Incomplete Utterance Rewriting	
Controllable generation	25 min
Mitigating hallucinations	
Controllable dataset generation	
Multilingual text editing	25 min
Tokenization	
Handling morphology	
Practical aspects	
Productionization	25 min
Latency	
Sample efficiency	
Recommendations and future directions	5 min
Total	180 min

Table 1: Tutorial structure and duration of each section.

1.1 Target Audience and Prerequisites

The tutorial is intended for researchers and practitioners who are familiar with generic seq2seq text-generation methods, such as Transformer (Vaswani et al., 2017) and pre-trained language models like BERT (Devlin et al., 2019). However, prior experience with text-editing models is not required to be able to follow the tutorial.

We expect the topic to attract people in both academia and industry. The high-sample efficiency and low-computational requirements of text-editing models (Malmi et al., 2019; Mallinson et al., 2020) makes them an attractive baseline, e.g., for researchers developing new text-generation tasks for which large training sets do not yet exist. Moreover, the high-inference speed of text-editing methods, owing to their often non-autoregressive architecture (Awasthi et al., 2019; Mallinson et al., 2020), makes them suitable for building real-time applications.

2 Tutorial Outline

The structure of the tutorial with duration estimates for different sections are shown in Table 1. Below we provide brief descriptions for each section.

Introduction. We first define the family of text-editing methods: Text-editing models are sequence-transduction methods that produce the output text by predicting edit operations which are applied to the inputs. In contrast, the traditional seq2seq methods produce the output from scratch, token by token. We summarize the main pros and cons of these two approaches and provide guidelines for choosing which approach is more suitable for a given task.

Model Design. The similarities and differences of a set of popular text-editing methods will be analyzed in terms of the types of edit operations they employ, their tagging architecture, and whether they are auto-regressive or feedforward. We also discuss methods for converting target texts into target edit sequences, a task which often does not have a unique solution. Table 2 provides a summary of the similarities and differences between the methods covered in the tutorial.

Applications. A key criterion for determining whether text-editing models are a good fit for a given application is the average degree of overlap between source and target texts. The higher the overlap, the more input tokens can be reused to generate the target, thus resulting in a simpler edit sequence. We give an overview of applications with a high degree of overlap to which text-editing methods have been applied to. Then we do a deep dive in to the following applications: grammatical error correction, text simplification, unsupervised style transfer, and incomplete utterance rewriting.

Controllable Generation. Text-editing models with a restricted vocabulary of phrases to insert (Malmi et al., 2019; Jin et al., 2022) or with linguistically informed suffix-transformation operations (Awasthi et al., 2019; Omelianchuk et al., 2020) are less prone to different types of hallucination since the models cannot produce arbitrary outputs. Moreover, the restricted vocabulary makes it feasible to manually refine the list of phrases that the model can insert. Another route through which the decomposition of the generation task into explicit edit operations can improve controllability is via biasing of certain types of edits to control how often the model will insert new text (Dong et al., 2019; Omelianchuk et al., 2020). Controllable generation with editing models can be useful for generating large synthetic datasets with a desired distribution of errors, which yields improvements in tasks such

Method	Non-autoregressive	Pre-trained decoder	Reordering	Unsupervised	Language-agnostic	Application(s)
EdiT5 (Mallinson et al., 2022)	(✓)	✓	✓		✓	*multiple*
EditNTS (Dong et al., 2019)					✓	Simplification
Felix (Mallinson et al., 2020)	✓	✓	✓		✓	*multiple*
GECToR (Omelianchuk et al., 2020)	✓	(✓)				GEC
HCT (Jin et al., 2022)	✓		✓		✓	Utterance Rewriting
LaserTagger (Malmi et al., 2019)	✓				✓	*multiple*
LevT (Gu et al., 2019)	(✓)	✓			✓	*multiple*
LEWIS (Reid and Zhong, 2021)		✓		✓	✓	Style Transfer
Masker (Malmi et al., 2020)	✓	✓		✓	✓	*multiple*
PIE (Awasthi et al., 2019)	✓	✓				GEC
Seq2Edits (Stahlberg and Kumar, 2020)					(✓)	*multiple*
SL (Alva-Manchego et al., 2017)	✓		✓		✓	Simplification

Table 2: Overview of selected text-editing methods.

as grammatical error correction (Stahlberg and Kumar, 2021). We will provide concrete examples of the aforementioned control measures and their effects.

Multilingual Text Editing. Most text-editing models, like text-generation models in general, are evaluated on English, but there are also methods evaluated or specifically developed for other languages, including Chinese (Hinson et al., 2020; Liu et al., 2020), Czech (Náplava and Straka, 2019), German (Mallinson et al., 2020), Russian (Stahlberg and Kumar, 2020), and Ukrainian (Syvokon and Nahorna, 2021). Apart from general tokenization-related challenges discussed in (Mielke et al., 2021), an additional challenge with applying text-editing methods to morphologically rich languages is a potential mismatch between the subword tokens, on which the underlying sequence labeling model operates, and the morphemes or affixes, on which the edits should happen. Possible solutions to this challenge include developing custom inflection operations (Awasthi et al., 2019; Omelianchuk et al., 2020) or learning them from the data (Straka et al., 2021), and using more fine-grained edit operations, such as character-level edits (Gao et al., 2021).

An additional challenge when building a truly multilingual model—as opposed to one model per language—is to ensure that it is not skewed towards a particular language or a set of languages (Chung et al., 2020) while being computationally efficient.

Productionization. We discuss how casting a text-generation problem as a text-editing task often allows the use of significantly faster and more data-efficient model architectures, without sacrificing output quality. We make use of the TensorFlow

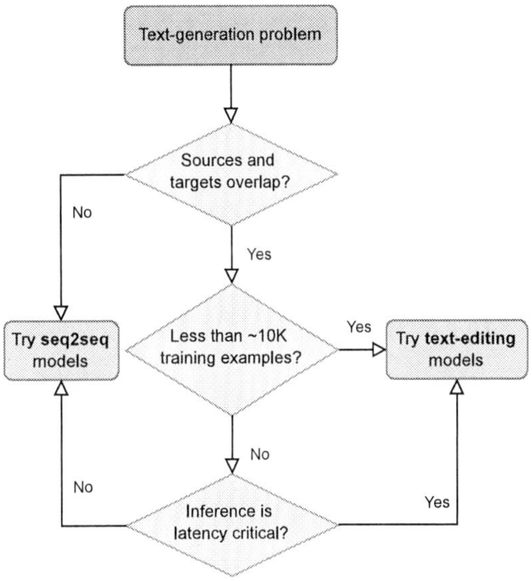

Figure 2: Proposed flowchart for deciding when to try a text-editing approach.

Profiler[2] to compare latencies of text-editing and non-text-editing solutions for an example problem, and illustrate where the time savings come from.

Recommendations and Future Directions. We provide practical guidelines for when to use (and when not to use) text-editing methods (see Figure 2 for a summary). We also outline possible future directions which include: (i) learned edit operations, (ii) studying the effects of different subword segmentation methods since these typically determine the granularity at which the edit operations are applied, (iii) text-editing-specific pre-training methods, (iv) sampling strategies for text-editing methods, and (v) studying the effects of scaling up

[2] https://www.tensorflow.org/guide/profiler#trace_viewer_interface

text-editing methods, a strategy that has been found to be very effective for many other text-generation methods (Brown et al., 2020; Chowdhery et al., 2022).

3 Diversity Considerations

A significant portion of the tutorial is devoted to discussing multilingual text-editing, including applying text-editing models to morphologically rich languages which presents specific challenges related to larger vocabularies and the need to edit word affixes. The presenters come from both academia and industry, are native speakers of 8 languages based in 4 different countries (Switzerland, Germany, Canada, USA), and are of different seniority levels from a PhD student to a Senior Staff Research Scientist.

4 Reading List

Before the tutorial, we expect the audience to read (Vaswani et al., 2017) and (Devlin et al., 2019). For references to text-editing works that will be discussed in the tutorial, see Table 2.

Breadth. 50% of the methods that will be discussed in the tutorial (cf. Table 2) are developed by different subsets of the tutorial instructors.

5 Presenters

Eric Malmi is a Senior Research Scientist at Google Switzerland. His research is focused on developing text-generation models for grammatical error correction and text style transfer. He received his PhD from Aalto University, Finland, where he also taught a course on Recent Advances in Natural Language Generation in Spring 2022.

Yue Dong is a final-year PhD student in CS at McGill University and Mila, Canada. Her research is focused on conditional text generation. She is a co-organizer for the NewSum workshop at EMNLP 2021 and ENLSP workshop at NeurIPS 2021.

Jonathan Mallinson is a Research Engineer at Google Switzerland. His research is focused on low-latency text-to-text generation. He received his PhD from the University of Edinburgh, Scotland.

Aleksandr Chuklin is a Research Engineer at Google Switzerland. His current research focuses on multi-lingual NLG. He organized workshops and conducted tutorials at conferences such as SIGIR, EMNLP, and IJCAI. Aleksandr received his PhD from University of Amsterdam, The Netherlands.

Jakub Adamek is a Research Engineer at Google Switzerland focusing on grammatical error correction and low-latency models. He received his MSc from Jagiellonian University.

Daniil Mirylenka is a Research Engineer at Google Switzerland working on text editing with application to grammatical error correction. He received his PhD from the University of Trento, Italy.

Felix Stahlberg is a Research Scientist at Google focusing on grammatical error correction and text style models. He received his PhD from Cambridge University, UK.

Sebastian Krause is a Senior Research Engineer at Google Switzerland. His work is focused on multi-lingual rewriting of questions in low-latency settings. Sebastian received his PhD in Engineering from the Technical University of Berlin, Germany.

Shankar Kumar is a Senior Staff Research Scientist at Google leading a research team working on speech and language algorithms. He received his PhD from the Johns Hopkins University, US.

Aliaksei Severyn is a Staff Research Scientist at Google Switzerland leading an applied research team working on next generation NLG solutions. He received his PhD from University of Trento, Italy.

6 Ethical Considerations

Text-generation methods have the potential to generate non-factual (Maynez et al., 2020; Pagnoni et al., 2021; Kreps et al., 2020) and offensive content (Gehman et al., 2020). Furthermore, training these models on uncurated data can lead to the models replicating harmful views presented in the training data (Bender et al., 2021). Text-editing models are also susceptible to these issues, but they have been shown to mitigate some of them. Specifically, they reduce the likelihood of different types of hallucination (Malmi et al., 2019) and their higher sample efficiency (Malmi et al., 2019; Mallinson et al., 2020) enables more careful curation of the training data. The tutorial will discuss the ethical issues related to text generation and provide concrete examples on how text-editing models can help mitigate them.

References

Sweta Agrawal, Weijia Xu, and Marine Carpuat. 2021. A non-autoregressive edit-based approach to controllable text simplification. In *Findings of the Association for Computational Linguistics: ACL-IJCNLP 2021*, pages 3757–3769, Online. Association for Computational Linguistics.

Fernando Alva-Manchego, Joachim Bingel, Gustavo Paetzold, Carolina Scarton, and Lucia Specia. 2017. Learning how to simplify from explicit labeling of complex-simplified text pairs. In *Proceedings of the Eighth International Joint Conference on Natural Language Processing (Volume 1: Long Papers)*, pages 295–305, Taipei, Taiwan. Asian Federation of Natural Language Processing.

Abhijeet Awasthi, Sunita Sarawagi, Rasna Goyal, Sabyasachi Ghosh, and Vihari Piratla. 2019. Parallel iterative edit models for local sequence transduction. In *Proceedings of the 2019 Conference on Empirical Methods in Natural Language Processing and the 9th International Joint Conference on Natural Language Processing (EMNLP-IJCNLP)*, pages 4260–4270, Hong Kong, China. Association for Computational Linguistics.

Dzmitry Bahdanau, Kyunghyun Cho, and Yoshua Bengio. 2015. Neural machine translation by jointly learning to align and translate. In *3rd International Conference on Learning Representations, ICLR 2015, San Diego, CA, USA, May 7-9, 2015, Conference Track Proceedings*.

Emily M Bender, Timnit Gebru, Angelina McMillan-Major, and Shmargaret Shmitchell. 2021. On the dangers of stochastic parrots: Can language models be too big? In *Proceedings of the 2021 ACM Conference on Fairness, Accountability, and Transparency*, pages 610–623.

Tom B. Brown, Benjamin Mann, Nick Ryder, Melanie Subbiah, Jared Kaplan, Prafulla Dhariwal, Arvind Neelakantan, Pranav Shyam, Girish Sastry, Amanda Askell, Sandhini Agarwal, Ariel Herbert-Voss, Gretchen Krueger, Tom Henighan, Rewon Child, Aditya Ramesh, Daniel M. Ziegler, Jeffrey Wu, Clemens Winter, Christopher Hesse, Mark Chen, Eric Sigler, Mateusz Litwin, Scott Gray, Benjamin Chess, Jack Clark, Christopher Berner, Sam McCandlish, Alec Radford, Ilya Sutskever, and Dario Amodei. 2020. Language models are few-shot learners. In *Advances in Neural Information Processing Systems 33: Annual Conference on Neural Information Processing Systems 2020, NeurIPS 2020, December 6-12, 2020, virtual*.

Mengyun Chen, Tao Ge, Xingxing Zhang, Furu Wei, and Ming Zhou. 2020. Improving the efficiency of grammatical error correction with erroneous span detection and correction. In *Proceedings of the 2020 Conference on Empirical Methods in Natural Language Processing (EMNLP)*, pages 7162–7169, Online. Association for Computational Linguistics.

Kyunghyun Cho, Bart van Merriënboer, Caglar Gulcehre, Dzmitry Bahdanau, Fethi Bougares, Holger Schwenk, and Yoshua Bengio. 2014. Learning phrase representations using RNN encoder–decoder for statistical machine translation. In *Proceedings of the 2014 Conference on Empirical Methods in Natural Language Processing (EMNLP)*, pages 1724–1734, Doha, Qatar. Association for Computational Linguistics.

Aakanksha Chowdhery, Sharan Narang, Jacob Devlin, Maarten Bosma, Gaurav Mishra, Adam Roberts, Paul Barham, Hyung Won Chung, Charles Sutton, Sebastian Gehrmann, et al. 2022. PaLM: Scaling Language Modeling with Pathways. *arXiv preprint arXiv:2204.02311*.

Hyung Won Chung, Dan Garrette, Kiat Chuan Tan, and Jason Riesa. 2020. Improving multilingual models with language-clustered vocabularies. In *Proceedings of the 2020 Conference on Empirical Methods in Natural Language Processing (EMNLP)*, pages 4536–4546, Online. Association for Computational Linguistics.

Jacob Devlin, Ming-Wei Chang, Kenton Lee, and Kristina Toutanova. 2019. BERT: Pre-training of deep bidirectional transformers for language understanding. In *Proceedings of the 2019 Conference of the North American Chapter of the Association for Computational Linguistics: Human Language Technologies, Volume 1 (Long and Short Papers)*, pages 4171–4186, Minneapolis, Minnesota. Association for Computational Linguistics.

Yue Dong, Zichao Li, Mehdi Rezagholizadeh, and Jackie Chi Kit Cheung. 2019. EditNTS: An neural programmer-interpreter model for sentence simplification through explicit editing. In *Proceedings of the 57th Annual Meeting of the Association for Computational Linguistics*, pages 3393–3402, Florence, Italy. Association for Computational Linguistics.

Mengyi Gao, Canran Xu, and Peng Shi. 2021. Hierarchical character tagger for short text spelling error correction. In *Proceedings of the Seventh Workshop on Noisy User-generated Text (W-NUT 2021)*, pages 106–113.

Samuel Gehman, Suchin Gururangan, Maarten Sap, Yejin Choi, and Noah A. Smith. 2020. RealToxicityPrompts: Evaluating neural toxic degeneration in language models. In *Findings of the Association for Computational Linguistics: EMNLP 2020*, pages 3356–3369, Online. Association for Computational Linguistics.

Jiatao Gu, Changhan Wang, and Junbo Zhao. 2019. Levenshtein transformer. In *Advances in Neural Information Processing Systems 32: Annual Conference on Neural Information Processing Systems 2019, NeurIPS 2019, December 8-14, 2019, Vancouver, BC, Canada*, pages 11179–11189.

Charles Hinson, Hen-Hsen Huang, and Hsin-Hsi Chen. 2020. Heterogeneous recycle generation for Chinese grammatical error correction. In *Proceedings of the 28th International Conference on Computational Linguistics*, pages 2191–2201, Barcelona, Spain (Online). International Committee on Computational Linguistics.

Lisa Jin, Linfeng Song, Lifeng Jin, Dong Yu, and Daniel Gildea. 2022. Hierarchical context tagging for utterance rewriting. In *Thirty-Sixth AAAI Conference on Artificial Intelligence, AAAI 2022*. AAAI Press.

Zdeněk Kasner and Ondřej Dušek. 2020. Data-to-text generation with iterative text editing. In *Proceedings of the 13th International Conference on Natural Language Generation*, pages 60–67, Dublin, Ireland. Association for Computational Linguistics.

Sarah Kreps, R Miles McCain, and Miles Brundage. 2020. All the news that's fit to fabricate: Ai-generated text as a tool of media misinformation. *Journal of Experimental Political Science*, pages 1–14.

Qian Liu, Bei Chen, Jian-Guang Lou, Bin Zhou, and Dongmei Zhang. 2020. Incomplete utterance rewriting as semantic segmentation. In *Proceedings of the 2020 Conference on Empirical Methods in Natural Language Processing (EMNLP)*, pages 2846–2857, Online. Association for Computational Linguistics.

Jonathan Mallinson, Jakub Adamek, Eric Malmi, and Aliaksei Severyn. 2022. Edit5: Semi-autoregressive text-editing with t5 warm-start. *arXiv preprint arXiv:2205.12209*.

Jonathan Mallinson, Aliaksei Severyn, Eric Malmi, and Guillermo Garrido. 2020. FELIX: Flexible text editing through tagging and insertion. In *Findings of the Association for Computational Linguistics: EMNLP 2020*, pages 1244–1255, Online. Association for Computational Linguistics.

Eric Malmi, Sebastian Krause, Sascha Rothe, Daniil Mirylenka, and Aliaksei Severyn. 2019. Encode, tag, realize: High-precision text editing. In *Proceedings of the 2019 Conference on Empirical Methods in Natural Language Processing and the 9th International Joint Conference on Natural Language Processing (EMNLP-IJCNLP)*, pages 5054–5065, Hong Kong, China. Association for Computational Linguistics.

Eric Malmi, Aliaksei Severyn, and Sascha Rothe. 2020. Unsupervised text style transfer with padded masked language models. In *Proceedings of the 2020 Conference on Empirical Methods in Natural Language Processing (EMNLP)*, pages 8671–8680, Online. Association for Computational Linguistics.

Joshua Maynez, Shashi Narayan, Bernd Bohnet, and Ryan McDonald. 2020. On faithfulness and factuality in abstractive summarization. In *Proceedings of the 58th Annual Meeting of the Association for Computational Linguistics*, pages 1906–1919, Online. Association for Computational Linguistics.

Sabrina J Mielke, Zaid Alyafeai, Elizabeth Salesky, Colin Raffel, Manan Dey, Matthias Gallé, Arun Raja, Chenglei Si, Wilson Y Lee, Benoît Sagot, et al. 2021. Between words and characters: A brief history of open-vocabulary modeling and tokenization in nlp. *arXiv preprint arXiv:2112.10508*.

Jakub Náplava and Milan Straka. 2019. Grammatical error correction in low-resource scenarios. In *Proceedings of the 5th Workshop on Noisy User-generated Text (W-NUT 2019)*, pages 346–356, Hong Kong, China. Association for Computational Linguistics.

Kostiantyn Omelianchuk, Vitaliy Atrasevych, Artem Chernodub, and Oleksandr Skurzhanskyi. 2020. GECToR – grammatical error correction: Tag, not rewrite. In *Proceedings of the Fifteenth Workshop on Innovative Use of NLP for Building Educational Applications*, pages 163–170, Seattle, WA, USA → Online. Association for Computational Linguistics.

Artidoro Pagnoni, Vidhisha Balachandran, and Yulia Tsvetkov. 2021. Understanding factuality in abstractive summarization with FRANK: A benchmark for factuality metrics. In *Proceedings of the 2021 Conference of the North American Chapter of the Association for Computational Linguistics: Human Language Technologies*, pages 4812–4829, Online. Association for Computational Linguistics.

Machel Reid and Victor Zhong. 2021. LEWIS: Levenshtein editing for unsupervised text style transfer. In *Findings of the Association for Computational Linguistics: ACL-IJCNLP 2021*, pages 3932–3944, Online. Association for Computational Linguistics.

Sascha Rothe, Jonathan Mallinson, Eric Malmi, Sebastian Krause, and Aliaksei Severyn. 2021. A simple recipe for multilingual grammatical error correction. In *Proceedings of the 59th Annual Meeting of the Association for Computational Linguistics and the 11th International Joint Conference on Natural Language Processing (Volume 2: Short Papers)*, pages 702–707, Online. Association for Computational Linguistics.

Felix Stahlberg and Shankar Kumar. 2020. Seq2Edits: Sequence transduction using span-level edit operations. In *Proceedings of the 2020 Conference on Empirical Methods in Natural Language Processing (EMNLP)*, pages 5147–5159, Online. Association for Computational Linguistics.

Felix Stahlberg and Shankar Kumar. 2021. Synthetic data generation for grammatical error correction with tagged corruption models. In *Proceedings of the 16th Workshop on Innovative Use of NLP for Building Educational Applications*, pages 37–47, Online. Association for Computational Linguistics.

Milan Straka, Jakub Náplava, and Jana Straková. 2021. Character transformations for non-autoregressive gec tagging. In *Proceedings of the Seventh Workshop on Noisy User-generated Text (W-NUT 2021)*, pages 417–422.

Ilya Sutskever, Oriol Vinyals, and Quoc V. Le. 2014. Sequence to sequence learning with neural networks. In *Advances in Neural Information Processing Systems 27: Annual Conference on Neural Information Processing Systems 2014, December 8-13 2014, Montreal, Quebec, Canada*, pages 3104–3112.

Oleksiy Syvokon and Olena Nahorna. 2021. Ua-gec: Grammatical error correction and fluency corpus for the ukrainian language.

Ashish Vaswani, Noam Shazeer, Niki Parmar, Jakob Uszkoreit, Llion Jones, Aidan N. Gomez, Lukasz Kaiser, and Illia Polosukhin. 2017. Attention is all you need. In *Advances in Neural Information Processing Systems 30: Annual Conference on Neural Information Processing Systems 2017, December 4-9, 2017, Long Beach, CA, USA*, pages 5998–6008.

Nikos Voskarides, Dan Li, Pengjie Ren, Evangelos Kanoulas, and Maarten de Rijke. 2020. Query resolution for conversational search with limited supervision. In *Proceedings of the 43rd International ACM SIGIR conference on research and development in Information Retrieval, SIGIR 2020, Virtual Event, China, July 25-30, 2020*, pages 921–930. ACM.

Tomasz Zietkiewicz. 2020. Post-editing and rescoring of asr results with edit operations tagging. In *Proceedings of the PolEval2020 Workshop*.

Self-supervised Representation Learning for Speech Processing

Hung-yi Lee[1] **Abdelrahman Mohamed**[2] **Shinji Watanabe**[3] **Tara Sainath**[4]
Karen Livescu[5] **Shang-Wen Li**[2] **Shu-wen Yang**[1] **Katrin Kirchhoff**[6]
[1]National Taiwan University [2]Facebook [3]Carnegie Mellon University
[4]Google [5]Toyota Technological Institute at Chicago [6]Amazon
hungyilee@ntu.edu.tw, {abdo, shangwel}@fb.com, shinjiw@ieee.org,
tsainath@google.com, klivescu@ttic.edu, katrinki@amazon.com, leo19941227@gmail.com

1 Introduction

There is a trend in the machine learning community to adopt self-supervised approaches to pre-train deep networks. Self-supervised representation learning (SSL) utilizes proxy supervised learning tasks, for example, distinguishing parts of the input signal from distractors, or generating masked input segments conditioned on the unmasked ones, to obtain training data from unlabeled corpora. BERT and GPT in NLP and SimCLR and BYOL in CV are famous examples in this direction. These approaches make it possible to use a tremendous amount of unlabeled data available on the web to train large networks and solve complicated tasks. Thus, SSL has the potential to scale up current machine learning technologies, especially for low-resourced, under-represented use cases, and democratize the technologies.

Recently self-supervised approaches for speech processing are also gaining popularity. There are several workshops in relevant topics hosted at ICML 2020[1], NeurIPS 2020[2], and AAAI 2022[3] [4]. We also found SSL for speech starting to be one of the focused topics in special/regular sessions of mainstream speech conferences such as ICASSP and Interspeech[5] [6]. On the other hand, there is a growing synergy between the speech and computational linguistic community because of the proximity of the two areas. Many problems including speech assistant, dialog management, speech translation, and automatic speech recognition attract researchers from both areas.

Due to the growing popularity of SSL, and the shared mission of the areas in bringing speech and language technologies to more use cases with better quality and scaling the technologies for under-represented languages, we propose this tutorial in the type of **Cutting-edge** to systematically survey the latest SSL techniques, tools, datasets, and performance achievement in speech processing. There is no previous tutorial about similar topic based on the authors' best knowledge. The tutorial aims to make the researchers in speech and language community aware of existing SSL innovation, and equipped to try out the new techniques. We also hope to bring researchers interested in the topics from both areas connected, catalyze new ideas and collaboration, and drive the SSL research frontier.

2 Tutorial Structure and Content

This is a three-hour tutorial. In the reference below, the red asterisks (*) indicate the papers of the speakers. This tutorial will cover at least 70% of the content not from the authors' papers.

2.1 Introduction and Motivation

We first introduce the general framework of pre-training SSL, and motivate the importance of SSL in speech processing. SSL makes it possible to leverage unlabeled audio data and avoid the costly data labeling step, which is especially helpful for low-resource languages.

2.2 Backgrounds and development trajectory

Representation learning is not an entirely new idea. This tutorial will briefly review what has been done before the wave of SSL in the speech community and the relations and differences between SSL and previous representation learning approaches. These approaches include clustering and mixture models (e.g., HMM, GMM) (Jansen and Church, 2011; Lee and Glass, 2012; Chung et al., 2013; Zhang and

[1]https://icml-sas.gitlab.io/
[2]https://neurips-sas-2020.github.io/
[3]https://aaai-sas-2022.github.io/
[4]Hung-yi Lee, Abdelrahman Mohamed, Shinji Watanabe, Tara Sainath, Karen Livescu, Shang-Wen Li are in the organization committee of the workshops at NeurIPS 2020 and AAAI 2022
[5]https://self-supervised-sp.github.io/Interspeech2020-Special-Session
[6]Organized by Hung-yi Lee, Abdelrahman Mohamed, Shinji Watanabe, Tara Sainath

Proceedings of the 2022 Conference of the North American Chapter of the Association for Computational Linguistics
Human Language Technologies: Tutorial Abstracts, pages 8 - 13
July 10-15, 2022

Glass, 2010), and stacked representation learners (e.g., RBM, NAE, NCE, SparseCoding) (Mohamed and Hinton, 2010)*(Driesen and Van hamme, 2012; Hazen et al., 2009; Sivaram et al., 2010).

2.3 Speech SSL Approaches

Then, we discuss the design and implementation details of existing speech SSL approaches, which can be categorized into three types, **Generative**, **Contrastive**, and **Predictive** approaches. **Generative** approaches learn SSL representations by reconstructing input features given historical or unmasked ones. Representative models in this type include APC (Chung et al., 2019; Chung and Glass, 2020a,b), VQ-APC (Chung et al., 2020), DeCoAR (Ling et al., 2020)*, DeCoAR 2.0 (Ling and Liu, 2020)*, Mockingjay (Liu et al., 2020; Chi et al., 2021)*, TERA (Liu et al., 2021b)*, MPC (Jiang et al., 2019, 2021), pMPC (Yue and Li, 2021), speech-XLNet (Song et al., 2020) NPC (Liu et al., 2021a), and PASE+ (Pascual et al., 2019; Ravanelli et al., 2020). **Contrastive** approaches pre-train representations to distinguish negative examples from real ones. Popular contrastive models consist of CPC (Oord et al., 2018), wav2vec (Schneider et al., 2019), vq-wav2vec (Baevski et al., 2020a), wav2vec 2.0 (Baevski et al., 2020b), and Wav2vec-c (Sadhu et al., 2021). **Predictive** approaches, such as HuBERT (Hsu et al., 2021)*, follow BERT pre-training through predicting discrete labels given input data.

In addition to the above three types, we will discuss the similarities and dissimilarities between SSL for speech and other modalities such as CV and NLP. We will also investigate studies in learning from multi-modal data as the naturally pairing of modalities in videos can potentially benefit representation learning without annotation. The discussion helps audience better connect works in adjacent communities and inspire more innovation.

2.4 Benchmarking, Toolkit, and Analysis

We will investigate existing benchmarks (e.g., SUPERB (wen Yang et al., 2021)*, LeBenchmark (Evain et al., 2021) and ZeroSpeech (Dunbar et al., 2020)) and analyses (e.g., (Pasad et al., 2021; wen Yang et al., 2020)*) for SSL speech models to understand their performance and what are encoded in representations. This tutorial will also include a demo to introduce the usage of the self-supervised speech representation toolkit: s3prl[7], and how to use s3prl in ESPNet[8], such that audiences interested in this research direction can try out their ideas easily.

2.5 From representation learning to zero resources

To illustrate the critical role of SSL in democratizing speech and language technologies for low-resourced use cases, we further discuss two topics, **unsupervised speech recognition** and **textless NLP**, and their relation to SSL. **Unsupervised speech recognition** (Liu et al., 2018; Chen et al., 2019)* (Yeh et al., 2018; ; Baevski et al., 2020b; Chung et al., 2018; Chung et al.) aims at solving speech recognition problem for the extremely low-resource languages, where only unpaired speech and text are available. We will discuss two research questions: 1) In such a situation, can machine still learn how to transcribe speech into text? 2) How can SSL models help unsupervised speech recognition?

Previously, connecting an NLP application to speech inputs meant that researchers had to first train an automatic speech recognition (ASR) system, which is available for just a handful of languages. The goal of **textless NLP** is to bring NLP and speech technology to languages that do not have ASR systems available or that do not even have written form, which contribute to around half of the languages in the world. In this topic, we will examine how to skip ASR and work in an end-to-end fashion, from the speech input to speech/text outputs, for scaling language and speech technologies to more languages (Polyak et al., 2021a,b)*.

2.6 Conclusion and future directions

We will conclude this tutorial with some possible future research directions. **Prompt Tuning**: As SSL models become larger, fine-tuning their parameters becomes challenging, which makes the idea of prompt tuning appealing. Prompt tuning has been widely studied for text (Liu et al., 2021c), but how to apply the technology to Speech SSL models is still unclear. **Small Footprint**: SSL speech models are usually gigantic. In order to make the technology more widely applicable, it is critical to develop small footprint SSL speech models. **Prevent Attack**: To build more robust SSL

[7]https://github.com/s3prl/s3prl
[8]https://github.com/espnet/espnet

speech models, how to prevent the models from all kinds of attacks, including adversarial attacks and privacy attacks, will be an important research question. **Bias issue**: Because the training data of SSL speech models is unlabeled, it is not trivial to control the distributions of the SSL training data. The influence of biased data on SSL speech models and impact of the biased models on downstream tasks are not sufficiently studied and might pose risk on the application of SSL.

3 Diversity

The proposed tutorial is highly relevant to the *special theme of ACL* about language diversity. One of the main focuses of the tutorial is leveraging SSL to reduce the dependence of speech and language technologies on labeled data, and to scale up the technologies especially for under-represented languages and use cases. We will also discuss the new challenges and ethical consideration brought by SSL to communities, such as heavy memory footprint, expensive computation for pre-training and inference, and carbon emission. These topics aim at stimulating discussion and investment in allowing more use cases, in terms of quantity and diversity, to benefit from the advancement of speech and language technologies with the application of SSL. Hence, ACL would be preferred because of the alignment of themes. NAACL-HLT/EMNLP/COLING are also acceptable due to the importance and relevance of SSL techniques for speech and language community.

In addition to the themes of tutorial, the presenters are also diverse in countries and genders. There are both senior and junior instructors, and come from academia and industry. With the diverse background of presenters, we aim to offer attendees a comprehensive review and encourage diversified discussion.

4 Attendee prerequisites and reading list

We will introduce every speech and language task discussed in the tutorial and require no domain knowledge about these tasks from attendees. Instead, the attendees should understand derivatives as found in introductory Calculus, possess basic knowledge in machine learning concepts such as classification, model optimization, gradient descent, pre-training, and Transformer. We also encourage the audience to read the papers of some well-known SSL techniques before the tutorial, which are listed below: (Ericsson et al., 2021; Rogers et al., 2020; Liu et al., 2021c; Qiu et al., 2020). Those papers focus on CV or NLP, so the content does not highly overlap with the tutorial, but the audience can learn more from the tutorial if they already have general ideas about SSL.

5 Tutorial Logistics

There is no previous tutorial on similar topics. Given our experiences from related ICML and NeurIPS workshops in 2020 (we observed 13 invited talks, 28 accepted papers, and over 150 participants combined) and the growing interests in SSL from academy, we estimate the number of participants to be between 100 and 200. We do not have special requirements for technical equipment and we will allow the publication of our slides and recording of the tutorial in the ACL Anthology.

6 Biographies of Presenters

Hung-yi Lee is an associate professor of the Department of Electrical Engineering of National Taiwan University, with a joint appointment at the Department of Computer Science & Information Engineering of the university. His research focuses on deep learning, spoken language understanding and speech recognition. He gave tutorials at ICASSP 2018[9], APSIPA 2018, ISCSLP 2018, INTERSPEECH 2019[10], SIPS 2019, INTERSPEECH 2020, ICASSP 2021, ACL 2021.

Abdelrahman Mohamed is a research scientist at Facebook AI research (FAIR) in Seattle. Before FAIR, he was a principal scientist/manager in Amazon Alexa AI team. From 2014 to 2017, he was in Microsoft Research Redmond. He received his PhD from the University of Toronto with Geoffrey Hinton and Gerald Penn where he was part of the team that started the Deep Learning revolution in Spoken Language Processing in 2009. He is the recipient of the IEEE Signal Processing Society Best Journal Paper Award for 2016. His research interests span Deep Learning, Spoken Language Processing, and Natural Language Understanding. He gave tutorials at the 4th International School on Deep Learning, and Facebook AI bootcamp in Dubai, UAE, 2021.

Shinji Watanabe is an Associate Professor at

[9]The tutorial has the most participants among the 14 tutorials in ICASSP 2018.

[10]The tutorial also has the most participants among the 8 tutorials in INTERSPEECH 2019.

Carnegie Mellon University. He was a research scientist at NTT Communication Science Laboratories, Kyoto, Japan, from 2001 to 2011, a visiting scholar in Georgia institute of technology, Atlanta, GA in 2009, and a senior principal research scientist at Mitsubishi Electric Research Laboratories (MERL), Cambridge, MA USA from 2012 to 2017. He was an associate research professor at Johns Hopkins University, Baltimore, MD USA from 2017 to 2020. His research interests include automatic speech recognition, speech enhancement, spoken language understanding, and machine learning for speech and language processing. He has published more than 200 papers in peer-reviewed journals and conferences and received several awards, including the best paper award from the IEEE ASRU in 2019. He served as an Associate Editor of the IEEE Transactions on Audio Speech and Language Processing. He was/has been a member of several technical committees, including the APSIPA Speech, Language, and Audio Technical Committee (SLA), IEEE Signal Processing Society Speech and Language Technical Committee (SLTC), and Machine Learning for Signal Processing Technical Committee (MLSP). He gave tutorials at ICASSP 2021, Interspeech 2019, APSIPA ASC 2016, Interspeech 2016, ICASSP 2012.

Tara Sainath received her PhD in Electrical Engineering and Computer Science from MIT in 2009. The main focus of her PhD work was in acoustic modeling for noise robust speech recognition. After her PhD, she spent 5 years at the Speech and Language Algorithms group at IBM T.J. Watson Research Center, before joining Google Research. She has co-organized a special session on Sparse Representations at Interspeech 2010 in Japan. In addition, she is a staff reporter for the IEEE Speech and Language Processing Technical Committee (SLTC) Newsletter. Her research interests are mainly in acoustic modeling, including deep neural networks, sparse representations and adaptation methods.

Karen Livescu is an Associate Professor at TTI-Chicago, a philanthropically endowed academic computer science institute located on the University of Chicago campus. She completed her PhD in 2005 at MIT in the Spoken Language Systems group of the Computer Science and Artificial Intelligence Laboratory. In 2005-2007 she was a post-doctoral lecturer in the MIT EECS department. Her main research interests are in speech and language processing and related problems in machine learning. Her recent work includes multi-view representation learning, acoustic word embeddings, visually grounded speech modeling, and automatic sign language recognition. Her recent professional activities include serving as a program chair of ICLR 2019 and a technical co-chair of ASRU 2015/2017/2019 and Interspeech 2022. She gave tutorials at SLT 2014, the Machine Learning Summer School, London, 2019, the Introduction to Machine Learning Summer School, Chicago, 2018, the Lisbon Machine Learning Summer School, Lisbon, 2018, Jelinek Summer Workshop School on Human Language Technology, 2015 and 2016.

Shang-Wen Li is a Research and Engineering Manager at Facebook AI, and he worked at Apple Siri, Amazon Alexa and AWS before joining Facebook. He completed his PhD in 2016 at MIT in the Spoken Language Systems group of Computer Science and Artificial Intelligence Laboratory (CSAIL). His research is focused on spoken language understanding, dialog management, machine reading comprehension, and low-resource speech processing. He gave 3-hour tutorials at INTERSPEECH 2020, ICASSP 2021, ACL 2021.

Shu-wen Yang is currently pursuing his Ph.D. degree in NTU. His research focuses on Self-Supervised Learning (SSL) in speech. He is dedicated to establishing the benchmark in this field, Speech processing Universal PERformance Benchmark (SUPERB), which focuses on SSL's generalizability across unseen data domains and tasks. He is also the co-creator of the S3PRL toolkit which includes numerous recipes for both pre-training and benchmarking for SSL in speech.

Katrin Kirchhoff is a Director of Applied Science at Amazon Web Services, where she heads several teams in speech and audio processing. Prior to joining Amazon she was a Research Professor at the University of Washington, Seattle, for 17 years, where she co-founded the Signal, Speech and Language Interpretation Lab. Her research interests are in speech processing, conversational AI, and machine learning, including representation learning, continual learning, and low-resource ASR. She has previously served on the editorial boards of Speech Communication and Computer, Speech, and Language, and was a member of the IEEE Speech Technical Committee.

References

Alexei Baevski, Steffen Schneider, and Michael Auli. 2020a. vq-wav2vec: Self-supervised learning of discrete speech representations. In *International Conference on Learning Representations*.

Alexei Baevski, Yuhao Zhou, Abdelrahman Mohamed, and Michael Auli. 2020b. wav2vec 2.0: A framework for self-supervised learning of speech representations. *Advances in Neural Information Processing Systems*, 33.

Kuan-Yu Chen, Che-Ping Tsai, Da-Rong Liu, Hung-Yi Lee, and Lin-shan Lee. 2019. Completely unsupervised speech recognition by a generative adversarial network harmonized with iteratively refined hidden markov models. *Proc. Interspeech 2019*, pages 1856–1860.

Po-Han Chi, Pei-Hung Chung, Tsung-Han Wu, Chun-Cheng Hsieh, Yen-Hao Chen, Shang-Wen Li, and Hung-yi Lee. 2021. Audio albert: A lite bert for self-supervised learning of audio representation. In *2021 IEEE Spoken Language Technology Workshop (SLT)*, pages 344–350.

Cheng-Tao Chung, Chun-an Chan, and Lin-shan Lee. 2013. Unsupervised discovery of linguistic structure including two-level acoustic patterns using three cascaded stages of iterative optimization. In *ICASSP*.

Yu-An Chung and James Glass. 2020a. Generative pre-training for speech with autoregressive predictive coding. In *ICASSP*.

Yu-An Chung and James Glass. 2020b. Improved speech representations with multi-target autoregressive predictive coding. In *ACL*.

Yu-An Chung, Wei-Ning Hsu, Hao Tang, and James Glass. 2019. An unsupervised autoregressive model for speech representation learning. *arXiv preprint arXiv:1904.03240*.

Yu-An Chung, Hao Tang, and James Glass. 2020. Vector-Quantized Autoregressive Predictive Coding. In *Interspeech*.

Yu-An Chung, Wei-Hung Weng, Schrasing Tong, and James Glass. Towards unsupervised speech-to-text translation. In *ICASSP*.

Yu-An Chung, Wei-Hung Weng, Schrasing Tong, and James Glass. 2018. Unsupervised cross-modal alignment of speech and text embedding spaces. *Advances in Neural Information Processing Systems*, 31:7354–7364.

Joris Driesen and Hugo Van hamme. 2012. Fast word acquisition in an NMF-based learning framework. In *ICASSP*.

Ewan Dunbar, Julien Karadayi, Mathieu Bernard, Xuan-Nga Cao, Robin Algayres, Lucas Ondel, Laurent Besacier, Sakriani Sakti, and Emmanuel Dupoux. 2020. The zero resource speech challenge 2020: Discovering discrete subword and word units. In *Interspeech*.

Linus Ericsson, Henry Gouk, Chen Change Loy, and Timothy M. Hospedales. 2021. Self-supervised representation learning: Introduction, advances and challenges.

Solène Evain, Ha Nguyen, Hang Le, Marcely Zanon Boito, Salima Mdhaffar, Sina Alisamir, Ziyi Tong, Natalia Tomashenko, Marco Dinarelli, Titouan Parcollet, Alexandre Allauzen, Yannick Estève, Benjamin Lecouteux, François Portet, Solange Rossato, Fabien Ringeval, Didier Schwab, and Laurent Besacier. 2021. LeBenchmark: A Reproducible Framework for Assessing Self-Supervised Representation Learning from Speech. In *Interspeech*.

Timothy J. Hazen, Wade Shen, and Christopher White. 2009. Query-by-example spoken term detection using phonetic posteriorgram templates. In *2009 IEEE Workshop on Automatic Speech Recognition Understanding*, pages 421–426.

Wei-Ning Hsu, Benjamin Bolte, Yao-Hung Hubert Tsai, Kushal Lakhotia, Ruslan Salakhutdinov, and Abdelrahman Mohamed. 2021. HuBERT: Self-supervised speech representation learning by masked prediction of hidden units. *arXiv preprint arXiv:2106.07447*.

Aren Jansen and Kenneth Church. 2011. Towards unsupervised training of speaker independent acoustic models. In *Interspeech*.

Dongwei Jiang, Xiaoning Lei, Wubo Li, Ne Luo, Yuxuan Hu, Wei Zou, and Xiangang Li. 2019. Improving transformer-based speech recognition using unsupervised pre-training. *arXiv preprint arXiv:1910.09932*.

Dongwei Jiang, Wubo Li, Ruixiong Zhang, Miao Cao, Ne Luo, Yang Han, Wei Zou, Kun Han, and Xiangang Li. 2021. A further study of unsupervised pretraining for transformer based speech recognition. In *ICASSP*.

Chia-ying Lee and James Glass. 2012. A nonparametric bayesian approach to acoustic model discovery. In *ACL*.

Shaoshi Ling and Yuzong Liu. 2020. Decoar 2.0: Deep contextualized acoustic representations with vector quantization. *arXiv preprint arXiv:2012.06659*.

Shaoshi Ling, Yuzong Liu, Julian Salazar, and Katrin Kirchhoff. 2020. Deep contextualized acoustic representations for semi-supervised speech recognition. In *ICASSP*.

Alexander H. Liu, Yu-An Chung, and James Glass. 2021a. Non-Autoregressive Predictive Coding for Learning Speech Representations from Local Dependencies. In *Interspeech*.

Andy T Liu, Shang-Wen Li, and Hung-yi Lee. 2021b. TERA: Self-supervised learning of transformer encoder representation for speech. *IEEE/ACM Transactions on Audio, Speech, and Language Processing*, 29:2351–2366.

Andy T Liu, Shu-wen Yang, Po-Han Chi, Po-chun Hsu, and Hung-yi Lee. 2020. Mockingjay: Unsupervised speech representation learning with deep bidirectional transformer encoders. In *ICASSP*.

Da-Rong Liu, Kuan-Yu Chen, Hung-Yi Lee, and Lin-shan Lee. 2018. Completely unsupervised phoneme recognition by adversarially learning mapping relationships from audio embeddings. *Proc. Interspeech 2018*, pages 3748–3752.

Pengfei Liu, Weizhe Yuan, Jinlan Fu, Zhengbao Jiang, Hiroaki Hayashi, and Graham Neubig. 2021c. Pre-train, prompt, and predict: A systematic survey of prompting methods in natural language processing.

Abdel-rahman Mohamed and Geoffrey Hinton. 2010. Phone recognition using restricted boltzmann machines. In *ICASSP*.

Aaron van den Oord, Yazhe Li, and Oriol Vinyals. 2018. Representation learning with contrastive predictive coding. *arXiv preprint arXiv:1807.03748*.

Ankita Pasad, Chou Ju-Chieh, and Livescu Karen. 2021. Layer-wise analysis of a self-supervised speech representation model. In *ASRU*.

Santiago Pascual, Mirco Ravanelli, Joan Serrà, Antonio Bonafonte, and Yoshua Bengio. 2019. Learning problem-agnostic speech representations from multiple self-supervised tasks. In *Interspeech*.

Adam Polyak, Yossi Adi, Jade Copet, Eugene Kharitonov, Kushal Lakhotia, Wei-Ning Hsu, Abdelrahman Mohamed, and Emmanuel Dupoux. 2021a. Speech resynthesis from discrete disentangled self-supervised representations.

Adam Polyak, Yossi Adi, Jade Copet, Eugene Kharitonov, Kushal Lakhotia, Wei-Ning Hsu, Abdelrahman Mohamed, and Emmanuel Dupoux. 2021b. Speech resynthesis from discrete disentangled self-supervised representations. In *Interspeech*.

XiPeng Qiu, TianXiang Sun, YiGe Xu, YunFan Shao, Ning Dai, and XuanJing Huang. 2020. Pre-trained models for natural language processing: A survey. *Science China Technological Sciences*, 63(10):1872–1897.

Mirco Ravanelli, Jianyuan Zhong, Santiago Pascual, Pawel Swietojanski, Joao Monteiro, Jan Trmal, and Yoshua Bengio. 2020. Multi-task self-supervised learning for robust speech recognition. In *ICASSP*.

Anna Rogers, Olga Kovaleva, and Anna Rumshisky. 2020. A primer in BERTology: What we know about how BERT works. *Transactions of the Association for Computational Linguistics*, 8:842–866.

Samik Sadhu, Di He, Che-Wei Huang, Sri Harish Mallidi, Minhua Wu, Ariya Rastrow, Andreas Stolcke, Jasha Droppo, and Roland Maas. 2021. wav2vec-C: A Self-Supervised Model for Speech Representation Learning. In *Interspeech*.

Steffen Schneider, Alexei Baevski, Ronan Collobert, and Michael Auli. 2019. wav2vec: Unsupervised pre-training for speech recognition. *arXiv preprint arXiv:1904.05862*.

G.S.V.S. Sivaram, Sridhar Krishna Nemala, Mounya Elhilali, Trac D. Tran, and Hynek Hermansky. 2010. Sparse coding for speech recognition. In *ICASSP*.

Xingchen Song, Guangsen Wang, Yiheng Huang, Zhiyong Wu, Dan Su, and Helen Meng. 2020. Speech-XLNet: Unsupervised Acoustic Model Pretraining for Self-Attention Networks. In *Interspeech*.

Shu wen Yang, Po-Han Chi, Yung-Sung Chuang, Cheng-I Jeff Lai, Kushal Lakhotia, Yist Y. Lin, Andy T. Liu, Jiatong Shi, Xuankai Chang, Guan-Ting Lin, Tzu-Hsien Huang, Wei-Cheng Tseng, Ko tik Lee, Da-Rong Liu, Zili Huang, Shuyan Dong, Shang-Wen Li, Shinji Watanabe, Abdelrahman Mohamed, and Hung yi Lee. 2021. SUPERB: Speech Processing Universal PERformance Benchmark. In *Interspeech*.

Shu wen Yang, Andy T. Liu, and Hung yi Lee. 2020. Understanding self-attention of self-supervised audio transformers. In *Interspeech*.

Chih-Kuan Yeh, Jianshu Chen, Chengzhu Yu, and Dong Yu. 2018. Unsupervised speech recognition via segmental empirical output distribution matching. *International Conference on Learning Representations*.

Xianghu Yue and Haizhou Li. 2021. Phonetically motivated self-supervised speech representation learning. *Interspeech*.

Yaodong Zhang and James R. Glass. 2010. Towards multi-speaker unsupervised speech pattern discovery. In *ICASSP*.

New Frontiers of Information Extraction

Muhao Chen[1], Lifu Huang[2], Manling Li[3], Ben Zhou[4], Heng Ji[3,5], Dan Roth[4,6]
[1]Department of Computer Science, USC
[2]Department of Computer Science, Virginia Tech
[3]Department of Computer Science, UIUC
[4]Department of Computer and Information Science, UPenn
[5]Alexa AI & [6]AWS AI Labs

Abstract

This tutorial targets researchers and practitioners who are interested in AI and ML technologies for structural information extraction (IE) from unstructured textual sources. In particular, this tutorial will provide audience with a systematic introduction to recent advances in IE, by addressing several important research questions. These questions include (i) how to develop a robust IE system from a small amount of noisy training data, while ensuring the reliability of its prediction? (ii) how to foster the generalizability of IE through enhancing the system's cross-lingual, cross-domain, cross-task and cross-modal transferability? (iii) how to support extracting structural information with extremely fine-grained and diverse labels? (iv) how to further improve IE by leveraging indirect supervision from other NLP tasks, such as Natural Language Generation (NLG), Natural Language Inference (NLI), Question Answering (QA) or summarization, and pre-trained language models? (v) how to acquire knowledge to guide inference in IE systems? We will discuss several lines of frontier research that tackle those challenges, and will conclude the tutorial by outlining directions for further investigation.

1 Introduction

Information extraction (IE) is the process of automatically extracting structural information from unstructured or semi-structured data. It provides the essential support for natural language understanding by recognizing and resolving the concepts, entities, events described in text, and inferring the relations among them. In various application domains, IE automates the costly acquisition process of domain-specific knowledge representations that have been the backbone of any knowledge-driven AI systems. For example, automated knowledge base construction has relied on technologies for entity-centric IE (Carlson et al., 2010; Lehmann et al., 2015). Extraction of events and event chains assists machines with narrative prediction (Zhang et al., 2021b; Chaturvedi et al., 2017) and summarization tasks (Liu et al., 2018; Chen et al., 2019b). Medical IE also benefits important but expensive clinical tasks such as drug discovery and repurposing (Sosa et al., 2019; Munkhdalai et al., 2018). Despite the importance, frontier research in IE still faces several key challenges. The first challenge is that existing dominant methods using language modeling representation cannot sufficiently capture the essential knowledge and structures required for IE tasks. The second challenge is on the development of extraction models for fine-grained information with less supervision, considering that obtaining structural annotation on unlabeled data has been very costly. The third challenge is to extend the reliability and generalizability of IE systems in real-world scenarios, where data sources often contain incorrect, invalid or unrecognizable inputs, as well as inputs containing unseen labels and mixture of modalities. By tackling those critical challenges, recent literature is leading to transformative advancement in principles and methodologies of IE system development. We believe it is necessary to present a timely tutorial to comprehensively summarize the new frontiers in IE research and point out the emerging challenges that deserve further investigation.

In this tutorial, we will systematically review several lines of frontier research on developing robust, reliable and adaptive learning systems for extracting rich structured information. Beyond introducing robust learning and inference methods for unsupervised denoising, constraint capture and novelty detection, we will discuss recent approaches for leveraging indirect supervision from natural language inference and generation tasks to improve IE. We will also review recent minimally supervised methods for training IE models with distant supervision from linguistic patterns, corpus statistics or language modeling objectives. In addition, we will

Proceedings of the 2022 Conference of the North American Chapter of the Association for Computational Linguistics Human Language Technologies: Tutorial Abstracts, pages 14 - 25
July 10-15, 2022

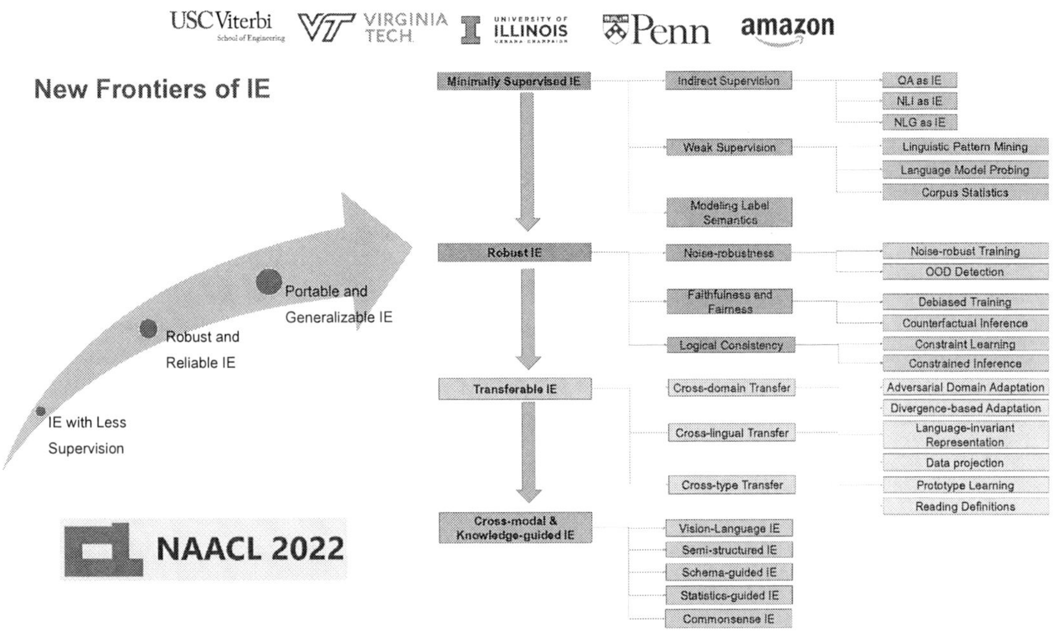

Figure 1: A roadmap for new frontiers of information extraction and a graphical abstract of this tutorial.

illustrate how a model trained on a close domain can be reliably adapted to produce extraction from data sources in different domains, languages and modalities, or acquiring global knowledge (e.g., event schemas) to guide the extraction on a highly diverse open label space. Participants will learn about recent trends and emerging challenges in this topic, representative tools and learning resources to obtain ready-to-use models, and how related technologies benefit end-user NLP applications. A graphical abstract of this tutorial is provided as Fig. 1, which serves as our roadmap for new frontiers of information extraction.

2 Outline of Tutorial Content

This **half-day** tutorial presents a systematic overview of recent advancement in IE technologies. We will begin motivating this topic with a selection of real-world applications and emerging challenges of IE. Then, we will introduce robust learning methods and inference methods to tackle noisy supervision, prediction inconsistency and out-of-distribution (OOD) inputs. We will also discuss about indirect supervision and minimal supervision methods that further improves IE model development under limited learning resources. Based on the robust IE systems developed in close-domain settings, we will explain how transfer learning technologies can adaptively extend the utility of the systems across domains, languages and tasks, and how complementary information can be extracted from data modalities other than human language. Moreover, we will exemplify the use of aforementioned technologies in various end-user NLP applications such as misinformation detection and scientific discovery, and will outline emerging research challenges that may catalyze further investigation on developing reliable and adaptive learning systems for IE. The detailed contents are outlined below.

2.1 Background and Motivation [20min]

We will define the main research problem and motivate the topic by presenting several real-world NLP and knowledge-driven AI applications of IE technologies, as well as several key challenges that are at the core of frontier research in this area.

2.2 Robust Learning and Inference for IE [35min]

We will introduce methodologies that enhance the robustness of learning systems for IE in both their learning and inference phases. Those methodologies involve self-supervised denoising techniques for training noise-robust IE models based on co-regularized knowledge distillation (Zhou and Chen, 2021; Liang et al., 2021), label re-weighting (Wang et al., 2019b) and label smoothing (Lukasik et al., 2020). Besides, we will also discuss about unsupervised techniques for out-of-distribution (OOD) detection (Zhou et al., 2021b; Hendrycks et al., 2020), prediction with abstention (Dhamija et al., 2018; Hendrycks et al., 2018) and novelty class detection (Perera and Patel, 2019) that seek to help the IE model identify invalid inputs or inputs with semantic shifts during its inference phase. Specifically, to demonstrate how models can ensure the global consistency of the extraction, we will cover constraint learning methods that automatically capture logical constraints among relations (Wang et al., 2021a, 2022c; Pan et al., 2020), and techniques to enforce the constraints in inference (Wang et al., 2020; Li et al., 2019a; Han et al., 2019; Lin et al., 2020). To assess if the systems give faithful extracts, we will also talk about the spurious correlation problems of current IE models and how to address them with counterfactual analysis (Wang et al., 2022b; Qian et al., 2021).

2.3 Minimally and Indirectly Supervised IE [35min]

We will introduce effective approaches that use alternative supervision sources for IE, that is, to use supervision signals from related tasks to make up for the lack of quantity and comprehensiveness in IE-specific training data. This includes indirect supervision sources such as question answering and reading comprehension (Wu et al., 2020; Lyu et al., 2021; Levy et al., 2017; Li et al., 2019b; Du and Cardie, 2020), natural language inference (Li et al., 2022a; Yin et al., 2020) and generation (Lu et al., 2021; Li et al., 2021b). We will also cover the use of weak supervision sources such as structural texts (e.g., Wikipedia) (Ji et al., 2017; Zhou et al., 2018) and global biases (Ning et al., 2018b). With the breakthrough of large-scale pretrained language models (Devlin et al., 2019; Li et al., 2022c), methodologies have been proposed to explore the language model objective as indirect supervision for IE. To this end, we will cover methods includes direct probing (Feldman et al., 2019; Zhang et al., 2020c), and more recently, pretraining with distant signals acquired from linguistic patterns (Zhou et al., 2020, 2021a).

2.4 Transferablity of IE Systems [35min]

One important challenge of developing IE systems lies in the limited coverage of predefined schemas (e.g., predefined types of entities, relations or events) and the heavy reliance on human annotations. When moving to new types, domains or languages, we have to start from scratch by creating annotations and re-training the extraction models. In this part of tutorial, we will cover the recent advances in improving the transferability of IE, including (1) cross-lingual transfer by leveraging adversarial training (Chen et al., 2019a; Huang et al., 2019; Zhou et al., 2019), language-invariant representations (Huang et al., 2018a; Subburathinam et al., 2019) and resources (Tsai et al., 2016; Pan et al., 2017), pre-trained multilingual language models (Wu and Dredze, 2019; Conneau et al., 2020) as well as data projection (Ni et al., 2017; Yarmohammadi et al., 2021), (2) cross-type transfer including zero-shot and few-shot IE by learning prototypes (Huang et al., 2018b; Chan et al., 2019; Huang and Ji, 2020), reading the definitions (Chen et al., 2020b; Logeswaran et al., 2019; Obeidat et al., 2019; Yu et al., 2022; Wang et al., 2022a), answering questions (Levy et al., 2017; Liu et al., 2020; Lyu et al., 2021), and (3) transfer across different benchmark datasets (Xia and Van Durme, 2021; Wang et al., 2021b). Finally, we will also discuss the progress on life-long learning for IE (Wang et al., 2019a; Cao et al., 2020; Yu et al., 2021; Liu et al., 2022) to enable knowledge transfer across incrementally updated models.

2.5 Cross-modal IE [20min]

Cross-modal IE aims to extract structured knowledge from multiple modalities, including unstructured and semi-structured text, images, videos, tables, etc. We will start from visual event and argument extraction from images (Yatskar et al., 2016; Gkioxari et al., 2018; Pratt et al., 2020; Zareian et al., 2020; Li et al., 2022b) and videos (Gu et al., 2018; Sadhu et al., 2021; Chen et al., 2021a). To extract multimedia events, the key challenge is to identify the cross-modal coreference and linking (Deng et al., 2018; Akbari et al., 2019; Zeng et al., 2019) and represent both text and visual knowledge in a common semantic space (Li et al., 2020a; Chen et al., 2021b; Zhang et al., 2021a; Li et al., 2022b). We will also introduce the information extraction from semi-structured data (Katti et al., 2018; Qian et al., 2019) and tabular data (Herzig et al., 2020).

2.6 Knowledge-guided IE [15min]

Global knowledge representation induced from large-scale corpora can guide the inference about the complicated connections between knowledge elements and help fix the extraction errors. We will introduce cross-task and cross-instance statistical constraint knowledge (Lin et al., 2020; Van Nguyen et al., 2021), commonsense knowledge (Ning et al., 2018a), and global event schema knowledge (Li et al., 2020b; Wen et al., 2021; Li et al., 2021a; Jin et al., 2022) that help jointly extract entities, relations, and events.

2.7 Future Research Directions [30min]

IE is a key component in supporting knowledge acquisition and it impacts a wide spectrum of knowledge-driven AI applications. We will conclude the tutorial by presenting further challenges and potential research topics in identifying trustworthiness of extracted content (Zhang et al., 2019, 2020b), IE with quantitative reasoning (Elazar et al., 2019; Zhang et al., 2020a), cross-document IE (Caciularu et al., 2021), incorporating domain-specific knowledge (Lai et al., 2021; Zhang et al., 2021c), extension to knowledge reasoning and prediction, modeling of label semantics (Huang et al., 2022; Mueller et al., 2022; Ma et al., 2022; Chen et al., 2020a), and challenges for acquiring implicit but essential information from corpora that potentially involve reporting bias (Sap et al., 2020).

3 Specification of the Tutorial

The proposed tutorial is considered a **cutting-edge** tutorial that introduces new frontiers in IE research. The presented topic has not been covered by ACL/EMNLP/NAACL/EACL/COLING tutorials in the past 4 years. One exception is the ACL 2020 tutorial "Multi-modal Information Extraction from Text, Semi-structured, and Tabular Data on the Web" that is partly relevant to one of our technical sections (§2.5). That particular section of our talk will focus on IE from visual and multi-media data in addition to semi-structured data, being different from the aforementioned ACL 2020 tutorial that has mainly covered topics on semi-structured data.

Audience and Prerequisites Based on the level of interest in this topic, we expect around 150 participants. While no specific background knowledge is assumed of the audience, it would be the best for the attendees to know about basic deep learning technologies, pre-trained word embeddings (e.g. Word2Vec) and language models (e.g. BERT). A reading list that could help provide background knowledge to the audience before attending this tutorial is given in Appx. §A.2.

Open Access All the materials are openly available at `https://cogcomp.seas.upenn.edu/page/tutorial.202207`.

4 Tutorial Instructors

The following are biographies of the speaker. Past tutorials given by us are listed in Appx. §A.1.

Muhao Chen is an Assistant Research Professor of Computer Science at USC, where he directs the Language Understanding and Knowledge Acquisition (LUKA) Group. His research focuses on data-driven machine learning approaches for natural language understanding and knowledge acquisition. His work has been recognized with an NSF CRII Award, a Cisco Faculty Research Award, an ACM SIGBio Best Student Paper Award, and a Best Paper Nomination at CoNLL. Muhao obtained his B.S. in Computer Science degree from Fudan University in 2014, his PhD degree from UCLA Department of Computer Science in 2019, and was a postdoctoral researcher at UPenn prior to joining USC. Additional information is available at `http://muhaochen.github.io`.

Lifu Huang is an Assistant Professor at the Computer Science department of Virginia Tech. He obtained a PhD in Computer Science from UIUC. He has a wide range of research interests in NLP, including extracting structured knowledge with limited supervision, natural language understanding and reasoning with external knowledge and commonsense, natural language generation, representation learning for cross-lingual and cross-domain transfer, and multi-modality learning. He is a recipient of the 2019 AI2 Fellowship and 2021 Amazon Research Award. Additional information is available at `https://wilburone.github.io/`.

Manling Li is a fourth-year Ph.D. student at the Computer Science Department of UIUC. Manling has won the Best Demo Paper Award at ACL'20, the Best Demo Paper Award at NAACL'21, C.L. Dave and Jane W.S. Liu Award, and has been selected as Mavis Future Faculty Fellow. She is a recipient of Microsoft Research PhD Fellowship. She has more than 30 publications on knowledge extraction and reasoning from multimedia data. Additional information is available at `https://limanling.github.io`.

Ben Zhou is a third-year Ph.D. student at the Department of Computer and Information Science, University of Pennsylvania. He obtained his B.S. from UIUC in 2019. Ben's research interests are distant supervision extraction and experiential knowledge reasoning, and he has more than 5 recent papers on related topics. He is a recipient of the ENIAC fellowship from the University of Pennsylvania, and a finalist of the CRA outstanding undergraduate researcher award. Additional information is available at `http://xuanyu.me/`.

Heng Ji is a Professor at Computer Science Department of University of Illinois Urbana-Champaign, and an Amazon Scholar. She received her B.A. and M. A. in Computational Linguistics from Tsinghua University, and her M.S. and Ph.D. in Computer Science from New York University. Her research interests focus on NLP, especially on Multimedia Multilingual Information Extraction, Knowledge Base Population and Knowledge-driven Generation. She was selected as "Young Scientist" and a member of the Global Future Council on the Future of Computing by the World Economic Forum. The awards she received include "AI's 10 to Watch" Award, NSF CAREER award, Google Research Award, IBM Watson Faculty Award, Bosch Research Award, and Amazon AWS Award, ACL2020 Best Demo Paper Award, and NAACL2021 Best Demo Paper Award. Additional information is available at `https://blender.cs.illinois.edu/hengji.html`.

Dan Roth is the Eduardo D. Glandt Distinguished Professor at the Department of Computer and Information Science, UPenn, the NLP Lead at AWS AI Labs, and a Fellow of the AAAS, ACM, AAAI, and ACL. In 2017 Roth was awarded the John McCarthy Award, the highest award the AI community gives to mid-career AI researchers. Roth was recognized "for major conceptual and theoretical advances in the modeling of natural language understanding, machine learning, and reasoning." Roth has published broadly in machine learning, NLP, KRR, and learning theory, and has given keynote talks and tutorials in all ACL and AAAI major conferences. Roth was the Editor-in-Chief of JAIR until 2017, and was the program chair of AAAI'11, ACL'03 and CoNLL'02; he serves regularly as an area chair and senior program committee member in the major conferences in his research areas. Prof. Roth received his B.A Summa cum laude in Mathematics from the Technion, and his Ph.D. in Computer Science from Harvard University in 1995. Additional information is available at `http://www.cis.upenn.edu/~danroth/`.

Acknowledgement

This presenters' research is supported in part by U.S. DARPA KAIROS Program No. FA8750-19-2-1004, DARPA AIDA Program No. FA8750-18-2-0014, DARPA MCS program No. N660011924033, and by the NSF of United States Grant IIS 2105329. The views and conclusions contained herein are those of the authors and should not be interpreted as necessarily representing the official policies, either expressed or implied, of DARPA, or the U.S. Government. The U.S. Government is authorized to reproduce and distribute reprints for governmental purposes notwithstanding any copyright annotation therein.

Ethical Considerations

Innovations in technology often face the ethical dilemma of dual use: the same advance may offer potential benefits and harms. For the IE technologies introduced in this tutorial, the distinction between beneficial use and harmful use depends mainly on the data. Proper use of the technology requires that input text corpora, as well as other modalities of inputs, are legally and ethically obtained. Regulation and standards provide a legal framework for ensuring that such data is properly used and that any individual whose data is used has the right to request its removal. In the absence of such regulation, society relies on those who apply technology to ensure that data is used in an ethical way. Besides, training and assessment data may be biased in ways that limit system accuracy on less well represented populations and in new domains, for example causing disparity of performance for different sub-populations based on ethnic, racial, gender, and other attributes. Furthermore, trained systems degrade when used on new data that is distant from their training data. Thus questions concerning generalizability and fairness need to be carefully considered when applying the IE technologies to specific datasets.

A general approach to ensure proper, rather than malicious, application of dual-use technology should: incorporate ethics considerations as the first-order principles in every step of the system design, maintain a high degree of transparency and interpretability of data, algorithms, models, and functionality throughout the system, make software available as open source for public verification and auditing, and explore countermeasures to protect vulnerable groups.

References

Hassan Akbari, Svebor Karaman, Surabhi Bhargava, Brian Chen, Carl Vondrick, and Shih-Fu Chang. 2019. Multi-level multimodal common semantic space for image-phrase grounding. In *Proceedings of the IEEE/CVF Conference on Computer Vision and Pattern Recognition*, pages 12476–12486.

Avi Caciularu, Arman Cohan, Iz Beltagy, Matthew E Peters, Arie Cattan, and Ido Dagan. 2021. Cdlm: Cross-document language modeling. In *Findings of ACL: EMNLP*.

Pengfei Cao, Yubo Chen, Jun Zhao, and Taifeng Wang. 2020. Incremental event detection via knowledge consolidation networks. In *Proceedings of the 2020 Conference on Empirical Methods in Natural Language Processing (EMNLP)*, pages 707–717.

Andrew Carlson, Justin Betteridge, Bryan Kisiel, Burr Settles, Estevam R Hruschka, and Tom M Mitchell. 2010. Toward an architecture for never-ending language learning. In *AAAI*.

Yee Seng Chan, Joshua Fasching, Haoling Qiu, and Bonan Min. 2019. Rapid customization for event extraction. In *Proceedings of the 57th Annual Meeting of the Association for Computational Linguistics: System Demonstrations*, pages 31–36.

Snigdha Chaturvedi, Haoruo Peng, and Dan Roth. 2017. Story comprehension for predicting what happens next. In *EMNLP*, pages 1603–1614.

Brian Chen, Xudong Lin, Christopher Thomas, Manling Li, Shoya Yoshida, Lovish Chum, Heng Ji, and Shih-Fu Chang. 2021a. Joint multimedia event extraction from video and article. In *Proc. The 2021 Conference on Empirical Methods in Natural Language Processing (EMNLP2021)*.

Brian Chen, Xudong Lin, Christopher Thomas, Manling Li, Shoya Yoshida, Lovish Chum, Heng Ji, and Shih-Fu Chang. 2021b. Joint multimedia event extraction from video and article. *EMNLP Findings*.

Muhao Chen, Hongming Zhang, Haoyu Wang, and Dan Roth. 2020a. "what are you trying to do?" semantic typing of event processes. In *Proceedings of the 24th Conference on Computational Natural Language Learning (CoNLL 2020)*. Association for Computational Linguistics.

Xilun Chen, Ahmed Hassan, Hany Hassan, Wei Wang, and Claire Cardie. 2019a. Multi-source cross-lingual model transfer: Learning what to share. In *Proceedings of the 57th Annual Meeting of the Association for Computational Linguistics*, pages 3098–3112.

Xiuying Chen, Zhangming Chan, Shen Gao, Meng-Hsuan Yu, Dongyan Zhao, and Rui Yan. 2019b. Learning towards abstractive timeline summarization. In *IJCAI*, pages 4939–4945.

Yunmo Chen, Tongfei Chen, Seth Ebner, Aaron Steven White, and Benjamin Van Durme. 2020b. Reading the manual: Event extraction as definition comprehension. In *Proceedings of the Fourth Workshop on Structured Prediction for NLP*, pages 74–83.

Alexis Conneau, Shijie Wu, Haoran Li, Luke Zettlemoyer, and Veselin Stoyanov. 2020. Emerging cross-lingual structure in pretrained language models. In *Proceedings of the 58th Annual Meeting of the Association for Computational Linguistics*, pages 6022–6034.

Chaorui Deng, Qi Wu, Qingyao Wu, Fuyuan Hu, Fan Lyu, and Mingkui Tan. 2018. Visual grounding via accumulated attention. In *Proceedings of the IEEE conference on computer vision and pattern recognition*, pages 7746–7755.

Jacob Devlin, Ming-Wei Chang, Kenton Lee, and Kristina Toutanova. 2019. Bert: Pre-training of deep bidirectional transformers for language understanding. In *NAACL*.

Akshay Raj Dhamija, Manuel Günther, and Terrance E Boult. 2018. Reducing network agnostophobia. In *NeurIPS*, pages 9175–9186.

Xinya Du and Claire Cardie. 2020. Event extraction by answering (almost) natural questions. In *Proceedings of the 2020 Conference on Empirical Methods in Natural Language Processing (EMNLP)*, pages 671–683.

Yanai Elazar, Abhijit Mahabaly, Deepak Ramachandran, Tania Bedrax-Weiss, and Dan Roth. 2019. How Large Are Lions? Inducing Distributions over Quantitative Attributes. In *Proc. of the Annual Meeting of the Association for Computational Linguistics (ACL)*.

Joshua Feldman, Joe Davison, and Alexander M. Rush. 2019. Commonsense knowledge mining from pretrained models. *EMNLP*.

Georgia Gkioxari, Ross Girshick, Piotr Dollár, and Kaiming He. 2018. Detecting and recognizing human-object interactions. In *Proceedings of the IEEE Conference on Computer Vision and Pattern Recognition*, pages 8359–8367.

Chunhui Gu, Chen Sun, David A Ross, Carl Vondrick, Caroline Pantofaru, Yeqing Li, Sudheendra Vijayanarasimhan, George Toderici, Susanna Ricco, Rahul Sukthankar, et al. 2018. Ava: A video dataset of spatio-temporally localized atomic visual actions. In *Proceedings of the IEEE Conference on Computer Vision and Pattern Recognition*, pages 6047–6056.

Rujun Han, Qiang Ning, and Nanyun Peng. 2019. Joint event and temporal relation extraction with shared representations and structured prediction. In *Proceedings of the 2019 Conference on Empirical Methods in Natural Language Processing and the 9th International Joint Conference on Natural Language Processing (EMNLP-IJCNLP)*, pages 434–444.

Dan Hendrycks, Xiaoyuan Liu, Eric Wallace, Adam Dziedzic, Rishabh Krishnan, and Dawn Song. 2020. Pretrained transformers improve out-of-distribution robustness. In *ACL*.

Dan Hendrycks, Mantas Mazeika, and Thomas Dietterich. 2018. Deep anomaly detection with outlier exposure. In *International Conference on Learning Representations*.

Jonathan Herzig, Pawel Krzysztof Nowak, Thomas Mueller, Francesco Piccinno, and Julian Eisenschlos. 2020. Tapas: Weakly supervised table parsing via pre-training. In *Proceedings of the 58th Annual Meeting of the Association for Computational Linguistics*, pages 4320–4333.

James Y. Huang, Bangzheng Li Li, Jiashu Xu, and Muhao Chen. 2022. Unified semantic typing with meaningful label inference. In *Proceedings of the 20th Annual Conference of the North American Chapter of the Association for Computational Linguistics (NAACL)*.

Lifu Huang, Kyunghyun Cho, Boliang Zhang, Heng Ji, and Kevin Knight. 2018a. Multi-lingual common semantic space construction via cluster-consistent word embedding. In *Proceedings of the 2018 Conference on Empirical Methods in Natural Language Processing*, pages 250–260.

Lifu Huang and Heng Ji. 2020. Semi-supervised new event type induction and event detection. In *Proceedings of the 2020 Conference on Empirical Methods in Natural Language Processing (EMNLP)*, pages 718–724.

Lifu Huang, Heng Ji, Kyunghyun Cho, Ido Dagan, Sebastian Riedel, and Clare Voss. 2018b. Zero-shot transfer learning for event extraction. In *Proceedings of the 56th Annual Meeting of the Association for Computational Linguistics (Volume 1: Long Papers)*, pages 2160–2170.

Lifu Huang, Heng Ji, and Jonathan May. 2019. Cross-lingual multi-level adversarial transfer to enhance low-resource name tagging. In *Proceedings of the 2019 Conference of the North American Chapter of the Association for Computational Linguistics: Human Language Technologies, Volume 1 (Long and Short Papers)*, pages 3823–3833.

Guoliang Ji, Kang Liu, Shizhu He, and Jun Zhao. 2017. Distant supervision for relation extraction with sentence-level attention and entity descriptions. In *AAAI*.

Xiaomeng Jin, Manling Li, and Heng Ji. 2022. Event schema induction with double graph autoencoders. In *Proc. The 2022 Conference of the North American Chapter of the Association for Computational Linguistics - Human Language Technologies (NAACL-HLT2022)*.

Anoop R Katti, Christian Reisswig, Cordula Guder, Sebastian Brarda, Steffen Bickel, Johannes Höhne, and Jean Baptiste Faddoul. 2018. Chargrid: Towards understanding 2d documents. In *Proceedings of the 2018 Conference on Empirical Methods in Natural Language Processing*, pages 4459–4469.

Tuan Lai, Heng Ji, ChengXiang Zhai, and Quan Hung Tran. 2021. Joint biomedical entity and relation extraction with knowledge-enhanced collective inference. In *Proc. The Joint Conference of the 59th Annual Meeting of the Association for Computational Linguistics and the 11th International Joint Conference on Natural Language Processing (ACL-IJCNLP 2021)*.

Jens Lehmann, Robert Isele, Max Jakob, Anja Jentzsch, Dimitris Kontokostas, Pablo N Mendes, Sebastian Hellmann, Mohamed Morsey, Patrick Van Kleef, Sören Auer, et al. 2015. Dbpedia–a large-scale, multilingual knowledge base extracted from wikipedia. *Semantic web*, 6(2):167–195.

Omer Levy, Minjoon Seo, Eunsol Choi, and Luke Zettlemoyer. 2017. Zero-shot relation extraction via reading comprehension. In *Proceedings of the 21st Conference on Computational Natural Language Learning (CoNLL 2017)*, pages 333–342.

Bangzheng Li, Wenpeng Yin, and Muhao Chen. 2022a. Ultra-fine entity typing with indirect supervision from natural language inference. *Transactions of the Association for Computational Linguistics*.

Manling Li, Sha Li, Zhenhailong Wang, Lifu Huang, Kyunghyun Cho, Heng Ji, and Jiawei Han. 2021a. The future is not one-dimensional: Complex event schema induction via graph modeling for event prediction. In *Proc. The 2021 Conference on Empirical Methods in Natural Language Processing (EMNLP2021)*.

Manling Li, Ruochen Xu, Shuohang Wang, Luowei Zhou, Xudong Lin, Chenguang Zhu, Michael Zeng, Heng Ji, and Shih-Fu Chang. 2022b. Clip-event: Connecting text and images with event structures. In *Proc. Conference on Computer Vision and Pattern Recognition (CVPR2022)*.

Manling Li, Alireza Zareian, Qi Zeng, Spencer Whitehead, Di Lu, Heng Ji, and Shih-Fu Chang. 2020a. Cross-media structured common space for multimedia event extraction. In *Proceedings of the 58th Annual Meeting of the Association for Computational Linguistics*, pages 2557–2568.

Manling Li, Qi Zeng, Ying Lin, Kyunghyun Cho, Heng Ji, Jonathan May, Nathanael Chambers, and Clare Voss. 2020b. Connecting the dots: Event graph schema induction with path language modeling. In *Proceedings of the 2020 Conference on Empirical Methods in Natural Language Processing (EMNLP)*, pages 684–695.

Sha Li, Heng Ji, and Jiawei Han. 2021b. Document-level event argument extraction by conditional generation. In *Proceedings of the 2021 Conference of the North American Chapter of the Association for Computational Linguistics: Human Language Technologies*, pages 894–908.

Sha Li, Liyuan Liu, Yiqing Xie, Heng Ji, and Jiawei Han. 2022c. Piled: An identify-and-localize framework for few-shot event detection. In *arXiv:2202.07615*.

Tao Li, Vivek Gupta, Maitrey Mehta, and Vivek Srikumar. 2019a. A logic-driven framework for consistency of neural models. In *EMNLP*.

Xiaoya Li, Fan Yin, Zijun Sun, Xiayu Li, Arianna Yuan, Duo Chai, Mingxin Zhou, and Jiwei Li. 2019b. Entity-relation extraction as multi-turn question answering. In *ACL*.

Xiaobo Liang, Lijun Wu, Juntao Li, Yue Wang, Qi Meng, Tao Qin, Wei Chen, Min Zhang, and Tie-Yan Liu. 2021. R-drop: Regularized dropout for neural networks. *arXiv preprint arXiv:2106.14448*.

Ying Lin, Heng Ji, Fei Huang, and Lingfei Wu. 2020. A joint neural model for information extraction with global features. In *Proceedings of the 58th Annual Meeting of the Association for Computational Linguistics*, pages 7999–8009.

Jian Liu, Yubo Chen, Kang Liu, Wei Bi, and Xiaojiang Liu. 2020. Event extraction as machine reading comprehension. In *Proceedings of the 2020 Conference on Empirical Methods in Natural Language Processing (EMNLP)*, pages 1641–1651.

Minqian Liu, Shiyu Chang, and Lifu Huang. 2022. Incremental prompting: Episodic memory prompt for lifelong event detection. *arXiv preprint arXiv:2204.07275*.

Zhengzhong Liu, Chenyan Xiong, Teruko Mitamura, and Eduard Hovy. 2018. Automatic event salience identification. In *EMNLP*, pages 1226–1236.

Lajanugen Logeswaran, Ming-Wei Chang, Kenton Lee, Kristina Toutanova, Jacob Devlin, and Honglak Lee. 2019. Zero-shot entity linking by reading entity descriptions. In *Proceedings of the 57th Annual Meeting of the Association for Computational Linguistics*, pages 3449–3460.

Yaojie Lu, Hongyu Lin, Jin Xu, Xianpei Han, Jialong Tang, Annan Li, Le Sun, Meng Liao, and Shaoyi Chen. 2021. Text2event: Controllable sequence-to-structure generation for end-to-end event extraction. In *ACL*.

Michal Lukasik, Srinadh Bhojanapalli, Aditya Menon, and Sanjiv Kumar. 2020. Does label smoothing mitigate label noise? In *ICML*, pages 6448–6458.

Qing Lyu, Hongming Zhang, Elior Sulem, and Dan Roth. 2021. Zero-shot event extraction via transfer learning: Challenges and insights. In *Proceedings of the 59th Annual Meeting of the Association for Computational Linguistics and the 11th International Joint Conference on Natural Language Processing (Volume 2: Short Papers)*, pages 322–332.

Jie Ma, Miguel Ballesteros, Srikanth Doss, Rishita Anubhai, Sunil Mallya, Yaser Al-Onaizan, and Dan Roth. 2022. Label semantics for few shot named entity recognition. In *Findings of the Association for Computational Linguistics: ACL 2022*, pages 1956–1971.

Aaron Mueller, Jason Krone, Salvatore Romeo, Saab Mansour, Elman Mansimov, Yi Zhang, and Dan Roth. 2022. Label semantic aware pre-training for few-shot text classification. In *Proceedings of the 60th Annual Meeting of the Association for Computational Linguistics (Volume 1: Long Papers)*, pages 8318–8334, Dublin, Ireland. Association for Computational Linguistics.

Tsendsuren Munkhdalai, Feifan Liu, Hong Yu, et al. 2018. Clinical relation extraction toward drug safety surveillance using electronic health record narratives: classical learning versus deep learning. *JMIR public health and surveillance*, 4(2):e9361.

Jian Ni, Georgiana Dinu, and Radu Florian. 2017. Weakly supervised cross-lingual named entity recognition via effective annotation and representation projection. In *Proceedings of the 55th Annual Meeting of the Association for Computational Linguistics (Volume 1: Long Papers)*, pages 1470–1480.

Qiang Ning, Zhili Feng, Hao Wu, and Dan Roth. 2018a. Joint reasoning for temporal and causal relations. In *Proceedings of the 56th Annual Meeting of the Association for Computational Linguistics (Volume 1: Long Papers)*, pages 2278–2288.

Qiang Ning, Hao Wu, Haoruo Peng, and Dan Roth. 2018b. Improving temporal relation extraction with a globally acquired statistical resource. In *NAACL*.

Rasha Obeidat, Xiaoli Fern, Hamed Shahbazi, and Prasad Tadepalli. 2019. Description-based zero-shot fine-grained entity typing. In *Proceedings of the 2019 Conference of the North American Chapter of the Association for Computational Linguistics: Human Language Technologies, Volume 1 (Long and Short Papers)*, pages 807–814.

Xiaoman Pan, Boliang Zhang, Jonathan May, Joel Nothman, Kevin Knight, and Heng Ji. 2017. Cross-lingual name tagging and linking for 282 languages. In *Proc. the 55th Annual Meeting of the Association for Computational Linguistics (ACL2017)*.

Xingyuan Pan, Maitrey Mehta, and Vivek Srikumar. 2020. Learning constraints for structured prediction using rectifier networks. In *ACL*, pages 4843–4858.

Pramuditha Perera and Vishal M Patel. 2019. Deep transfer learning for multiple class novelty detection. In *CVPR*, pages 11544–11552.

Sarah Pratt, Mark Yatskar, Luca Weihs, Ali Farhadi, and Aniruddha Kembhavi. 2020. Grounded situation recognition. In *European Conference on Computer Vision*, pages 314–332. Springer.

Chen Qian, Fuli Feng, Lijie Wen, Chunping Ma, and Pengjun Xie. 2021. Counterfactual inference for text classification debiasing. In *Proceedings of the 59th Annual Meeting of the Association for Computational Linguistics and the 11th International Joint Conference on Natural Language Processing (Volume 1: Long Papers)*, pages 5434–5445.

Yujie Qian, Enrico Santus, Zhijing Jin, Jiang Guo, and Regina Barzilay. 2019. Graphie: A graph-based framework for information extraction. In *Proceedings of the 2019 Conference of the North American Chapter of the Association for Computational Linguistics: Human Language Technologies, Volume 1 (Long and Short Papers)*, pages 751–761.

Arka Sadhu, Tanmay Gupta, Mark Yatskar, Ram Nevatia, and Aniruddha Kembhavi. 2021. Visual semantic role labeling for video understanding. In *Proceedings of the IEEE/CVF Conference on Computer Vision and Pattern Recognition*, pages 5589–5600.

Maarten Sap, Vered Shwartz, Antoine Bosselut, Yejin Choi, and Dan Roth. 2020. Commonsense reasoning for natural language processing. In *ACL: Tutorial Abstracts*, pages 27–33.

Daniel N Sosa, Alexander Derry, Margaret Guo, Eric Wei, Connor Brinton, and Russ B Altman. 2019. A literature-based knowledge graph embedding method for identifying drug repurposing opportunities in rare diseases. In *PSB*, pages 463–474.

Ananya Subburathinam, Di Lu, Heng Ji, Jonathan May, Shih-Fu Chang, Avirup Sil, and Clare Voss. 2019. Cross-lingual structure transfer for relation and event extraction. In *Proceedings of the 2019 Conference on Empirical Methods in Natural Language Processing and the 9th International Joint Conference on Natural Language Processing (EMNLP-IJCNLP)*, pages 313–325.

Chen-Tse Tsai, Stephen Mayhew, and Dan Roth. 2016. Cross-lingual named entity recognition via wikification. In *Proceedings of The 20th SIGNLL Conference on Computational Natural Language Learning*, pages 219–228.

Minh Van Nguyen, Viet Lai, and Thien Huu Nguyen. 2021. Cross-task instance representation interactions and label dependencies for joint information extraction with graph convolutional networks. In *Proceedings of the 2021 Conference of the North American Chapter of the Association for Computational Linguistics: Human Language Technologies*, pages 27–38.

Haoyu Wang, Muhao Chen, Hongming Zhang, and Dan Roth. 2020. Joint constrained learning for event-event relation extraction. In *EMNLP*.

Haoyu Wang, Hongming Zhang, Muhao Chen, and Dan Roth. 2021a. Learning constraints and descriptive segmentation for subevent detection. In *EMNLP*.

Hong Wang, Wenhan Xiong, Mo Yu, Xiaoxiao Guo, Shiyu Chang, and William Yang Wang. 2019a. Sentence embedding alignment for lifelong relation extraction. In *Proceedings of the 2019 Conference of the North American Chapter of the Association for Computational Linguistics: Human Language Technologies, Volume 1 (Long and Short Papers)*, pages 796–806.

Sijia Wang, Mo Yu, Shiyu Chang, Lichao Sun, and Lifu Huang. 2021b. Query and extract: Refining event extraction as type-oriented binary decoding. *arXiv preprint arXiv:2110.07476*.

Sijia Wang, Mo Yu, and Lifu Huang. 2022a. The art of prompting: Event detection based on type specific prompts. *arXiv preprint arXiv:2204.07241*.

Yiwei Wang, Muhao Chen, Wenxuan Zhou, Yujun Cai, Yuxuan Liang, Dayiheng Liu Liu, Baosong Yang, Juncheng Liu, and Bryan Hooi. 2022b. Should we rely on entity mentions for relation extraction? debiasing relation extraction with counterfactual analysis. In *Proceedings of the 20th Annual Conference of the North American Chapter of the Association for Computational Linguistics (NAACL)*.

Yiwei Wang, Muhao Chen, Wenxuan Zhou Zhou, Yujun Cai Cai, Yuxuan Liang, and Bryan Hooi. 2022c. Graphcache: Message passing as caching for sentence-level relation extraction. In *Findings of NAACL*.

Zihan Wang, Jingbo Shang, Liyuan Liu, Lihao Lu, Jiacheng Liu, and Jiawei Han. 2019b. CrossWeigh: Training named entity tagger from imperfect annotations. In *EMNLP*, pages 5154–5163, Hong Kong, China.

Haoyang Wen, Ying Lin, Tuan Lai, Xiaoman Pan, Sha Li, Xudong Lin, Ben Zhou, Manling Li, Haoyu Wang, Hongming Zhang, et al. 2021. Resin: A dockerized schema-guided cross-document cross-lingual cross-media information extraction and event tracking system. In *Proceedings of the 2021 Conference of the North American Chapter of the Association for Computational Linguistics: Human Language Technologies: Demonstrations*, pages 133–143.

Shijie Wu and Mark Dredze. 2019. Beto, bentz, becas: The surprising cross-lingual effectiveness of bert. In *Proceedings of the 2019 Conference on Empirical Methods in Natural Language Processing and the 9th International Joint Conference on Natural Language Processing (EMNLP-IJCNLP)*, pages 833–844.

Wei Wu, Fei Wang, Arianna Yuan, Fei Wu, and Jiwei Li. 2020. CorefQA: Coreference resolution as query-based span prediction. In *Proceedings of the 58th Annual Meeting of the Association for Computational Linguistics*, pages 6953–6963, Online. Association for Computational Linguistics.

Patrick Xia and Benjamin Van Durme. 2021. Moving on from ontonotes: Coreference resolution model transfer. *arXiv preprint arXiv:2104.08457*.

Mahsa Yarmohammadi, Shijie Wu, Marc Marone, Haoran Xu, Seth Ebner, Guanghui Qin, Yunmo Chen, Jialiang Guo, Craig Harman, Kenton Murray, et al. 2021. Everything is all it takes: A multipronged strategy for zero-shot cross-lingual information extraction. *arXiv preprint arXiv:2109.06798*.

Mark Yatskar, Luke Zettlemoyer, and Ali Farhadi. 2016. Situation recognition: Visual semantic role labeling for image understanding. In *Proceedings of the IEEE conference on computer vision and pattern recognition*, pages 5534–5542.

Wenpeng Yin, Nazneen Fatema Rajani, Dragomir Radev, Richard Socher, and Caiming Xiong. 2020. Universal natural language processing with limited annotations: Try few-shot textual entailment as a start. In *EMNLP*, pages 8229–8239.

Pengfei Yu, Heng Ji, and Premkumar Natarajan. 2021. Lifelong event detection with knowledge transfer. In *Proc. The 2021 Conference on Empirical Methods in Natural Language Processing (EMNLP2021)*.

Pengfei Yu, Zixuan Zhang, Clare Voss, Jonathan May, and Heng Ji. 2022. Event extractor with only a few examples. In *Proc. NAACL2022 workshop on Deep Learning for Low Resource NLP*.

Alireza Zareian, Svebor Karaman, and Shih-Fu Chang. 2020. Weakly supervised visual semantic parsing. In *Proceedings of the IEEE/CVF Conference on Computer Vision and Pattern Recognition*, pages 3736–3745.

Runhao Zeng, Wenbing Huang, Mingkui Tan, Yu Rong, Peilin Zhao, Junzhou Huang, and Chuang Gan. 2019. Graph convolutional networks for temporal action localization. In *Proceedings of the IEEE/CVF International Conference on Computer Vision*, pages 7094–7103.

Linhai Zhang, Deyu Zhou, Yulan He, and Zeng Yang. 2021a. Merl: Multimodal event representation learning in heterogeneous embedding spaces. In *Proceedings of the AAAI Conference on Artificial Intelligence*, volume 35, pages 14420–14427.

Xikun Zhang, Deepak Ramachandran, Ian Tenney, Yanai Elazar, and Dan Roth. 2020a. Do language embeddings capture scales? In *Proceedings of the 2020 Conference on Empirical Methods in Natural Language Processing: Findings*, pages 4889–4896.

Xiyang Zhang, Muhao Chen, and Jonathan May. 2021b. Salience-aware event chain modeling for narrative understanding. In *EMNLP*.

Yi Zhang, Zachary Ives, and Dan Roth. 2019. Evidence-based trustworthiness. In *ACL*, pages 413–423.

Yi Zhang, Zachary G. Ives, and Dan Roth. 2020b. "Who said it, and Why?" Provenance for Natural Language Claims. In *Proc. of the Annual Meeting of the Association for Computational Linguistics (ACL)*.

Yunyi Zhang, Jiaming Shen, Jingbo Shang, and Jiawei Han. 2020c. Empower entity set expansion via language model probing. *ACL*.

Zixuan Zhang, Nikolaus Nova Parulian, Heng Ji, Ahmed S. Elsayed, Skatje Myers, and Martha Palmer. 2021c. Biomedical information extraction based on knowledge-enriched abstract meaning representation. In *Proc. The Joint Conference of the 59th Annual Meeting of the Association for Computational Linguistics and the 11th International Joint Conference on Natural Language Processing (ACL-IJCNLP 2021)*.

Ben Zhou, Daniel Khashabi, Chen-Tse Tsai, and Dan Roth. 2018. Zero-shot open entity typing as type-compatible grounding. In *EMNLP*.

Ben Zhou, Qiang Ning, Daniel Khashabi, and Dan Roth. 2020. Temporal common sense acquisition with minimal supervision. *ACL*.

Ben Zhou, Kyle Richardson, Qiang Ning, Tushar Khot, Ashish Sabharwal, and Dan Roth. 2021a. Temporal reasoning on implicit events from distant supervision. *NAACL*.

Joey Tianyi Zhou, Hao Zhang, Di Jin, Hongyuan Zhu, Meng Fang, Rick Siow Mong Goh, and Kenneth Kwok. 2019. Dual adversarial neural transfer for low-resource named entity recognition. In *Proceedings of the 57th Annual Meeting of the Association for Computational Linguistics*, pages 3461–3471.

Wenxuan Zhou and Muhao Chen. 2021. Learning from noisy labels for entity-centric information extraction. In *EMNLP*.

Wenxuan Zhou, Fangyu Liu, and Muhao Chen. 2021b. Contrastive out-of-distribution detection for pretrained transformers. In *EMNLP*.

A Appendix

A.1 Past Tutorials by the Instructors

The presenters of this tutorial have given the following tutorials at leading international conferences and venues in the past:

- Muhao Chen:

- ACL'21: Event-Centric Natural Language Processing.
- AAAI'21: Event-Centric Natural Language Understanding.
- KDD'21: From Tables to Knowledge: Recent Advances in Table Understanding.
- AAAI'20: Recent Advances of Transferable Representation Learning.

• Manling Li:

- ACL'21: Event-Centric Natural Language Processing.
- AAAI'21: Event-Centric Natural Language Understanding.

• Heng Ji:

- KDD'22: The Battlefront of Combating Misinformation and Coping with Media Bias.
- AACL'22: The Battlefront of Combating Misinformation and Coping with Media Bias.
- KDD'22: New Frontiers of Scientific Text Mining: Tasks, Data, and Tools.
- WWW'22: Modern Natural Language Processing Techniques for Scientific Web Mining: Tasks, Data, and Tools.
- AAAI'22: Deep Learning on Graphs for Natural Language Processing.
- KDD'21: Deep Learning on Graphs for Natural Language Processing.
- IJCAI'21: Deep Learning on Graphs for Natural Language Processing.
- SIGIR'21: Deep Learning on Graphs for Natural Language Processing.
- EMNLP'21: Knowledge-Enriched Natural Language Generation.
- ACL'21: Event-Centric Natural Language Processing.
- NAACL'21: Deep Learning on Graphs for Natural Language Processing.
- AAAI'21: Event-Centric Natural Language Understanding.
- CCL'18 and NLP-NADB'18: Multi-lingual Entity Discovery and Linking.
- ACL'18: Multi-lingual Entity Discovery and Linking.
- SIGMOD'16: Automatic Entity Recognition and Typing in Massive Text Data.
- ACL'15: Successful Data Mining Methods for NLP.
- ACL'14: Wikification and Beyond: The Challenges of Entity and Concept Grounding.
- NLPCC'14: Wikification and Beyond: The Challenges of Entity and Concept Grounding.
- COLING'12: Temporal Information Extraction and Shallow Temporal Reasoning.

• Dan Roth:

- ACL'21: Event-Centric Natural Language Processing.
- AAAI'21: Event-Centric Natural Language Understanding.
- ACL'20: Commonsense Reasoning for Natural Language Processing.
- AAAI'20: Recent Advances of Transferable Representation Learning.
- ACL'18: A tutorial on Multi-lingual Entity Discovery and Linking.
- EACL'17: A tutorial on Integer Linear Programming Formulations in Natural Language Processing.
- AAAI'16: A tutorial on Structured Prediction.
- ACL'14: A tutorial on Wikification and Entity Linking.
- AAAI'13: Information Trustworthiness.
- COLING'12: A Tutorial on Temporal Information Extraction and Shallow Temporal Reasoning.
- NAACL'12: A Tutorial on Constrained Conditional Models: Structured Predictions in NLP.
- NAACL'10: A Tutorial on Integer Linear Programming Methods in NLP.
- EACL'09: A Tutorial on Constrained Conditional Models.
- ACL'07: A Tutorial on Textual Entailment.

A.2 Recommended Paper List

The following is a reading list that could help provide background knowledge to the audience before attending this tutorial:

• Wenxuan Zhou, Muhao Chen. Learning from Noisy Labels for Entity-Centric Information Extraction. EMNLP, 2021.

• Wenxuan Zhou, Fanyu Liu, Muhao Chen. Contrastive Out-of-Distribution Detection for Pretrained Transformers. EMNLP, 2021.

• Xingyuan Pan, Maitrey Mehta, Vivek Srikumar. Learning Constraints for Structured Prediction Using Rectifier Networks. ACL, 2020.

- Hangfeng He, Mingyuan Zhang, Qiang Ning, Dan Roth. Foreseeing the Benefits of Incidental Supervision. EMNLP, 2021.
- Ben Zhou, Qiang Ning, Daniel Khashabi, Dan Roth. Temporal Common Sense Acquisition with Minimal Supervision. ACL, 2020.
- Wenpeng Yin, Nazneen Fatema Rajani, Dragomir Radev, Richard Socher, Caiming Xiong. Universal natural language processing with limited annotations: Try few-shot textual entailment as astart. EMNLP, 2020.
- Bangzheng Li, Wenpeng Yin, Muhao Chen. Ultra-fine Entity Typing with Indirect Supervision from Natural Language Inference. TACL, 2022.
- Lifu Huang, Heng Ji, Kyunghyun Cho, Ido Dagan, Sebastian Riedel, Clare Voss. Zero-shot transfer learning for event extraction. ACL, 2018.
- Ananya Subburathinam, Di Lu, Heng Ji, Jonathan May, Shih-Fu Chang, Avirup Sil, Clare Voss. Cross-lingual structure transfer for relation and event extraction. EMNLP, 2019.
- Hong Wang, Wenhan Xiong, Mo Yu, Xiaoxiao Guo, Shiyu Chang, William Yang Wang. Sentence Embedding Alignment for Lifelong Relation Extraction. NAACL, 2019.
- Hassan Akbari, Svebor Karaman, Surabhi Bhargava, Brian Chen, Carl Vondrick, and Shih-Fu Chang. Multi-level multimodal common semantic space for image-phrase grounding. CVPR, 2019.
- Manling Li, Alireza Zareian, Qi Zeng, Spencer Whitehead, Di Lu, Heng Ji, Shih-Fu Chang. Cross-media structured common space for multimedia event extraction. ACL, 2020.

Human-Centered Evaluation of Explanations

Jordan Boyd-Graber[1], **Samuel Carton**[2,3], **Shi Feng**[3], **Q. Vera Liao**[4],
Tania Lombrozo[5], **Alison Smith-Renner**[6], **Chenhao Tan**[3]
[1]University of Maryland, [2]University of New Hampshire, [3]University of Chicago,
[4]Microsoft Research, [5]Princeton University, [6]Dataminr

Abstract

The NLP community are increasingly interested in providing explanations for NLP models to help people make sense of model behavior and potentially improve human interaction with models. In addition to computational challenges in generating these explanations, evaluations of the generated explanations require human-centered perspectives and approaches. This tutorial will provide an overview of human-centered evaluations of explanations. First, we will give a brief introduction to the psychological foundation of explanations as well as types of NLP model explanations and their corresponding presentation, to provide the necessary background. We will then present a taxonomy of human-centered evaluation of explanations and dive into depth in the two categories: 1) evaluation with human-subjects studies; 2) evaluation based on human-annotated explanations. We will conclude by discussing future directions. We will also adopt *a flipped format* to maximize the interactive components for the live audience.

Type of Tutorial: It will be designed to provide introductory content for computer scientists, but aim to cultivate cutting-edge interdisciplinary research to work on this inherently human-centric topic by introducing perspectives and methods from psychology and human-computer interaction (HCI).

1 Tutorial Description

Thanks to recent advances in deep learning and large-scale pretrained language models, NLP systems have demonstrated impressive performance in a wide variety of tasks, ranging from classification to generation. However, in order to effectively use these NLP systems in support of human endeavour, it is critical that we can explain model predictions in ways that humans can easily comprehend. Such explanations are particularly important for high-stakes decisions such as hiring and loan approval. Indeed, the NLP community have developed a battery of algorithms and models for explaining model predictions and there have been past tutorials dedicated to such algorithms (Wallace et al., 2020).

However, there is less consensus on how to evaluate explanations. And, since these explanations eventually serve the needs of humans, it is important to take a human-centered approach to their evaluation, meaning evaluating with respect to human criteria, measuring human perceptions of explanations and whether explanations serve human needs. Therefore, interdiscplinary perspectives are necessary for the success of such evaluations, especially ones from psychology and HCI, which is unfamiliar to the NLP community. This tutorial aims to fill in this gap and introduce the nascent area of human-centered evaluation of explanations.

This tutorial will first present the psychological and philosophical foundations of explanations. We will highlight that explanations are heterogeneous and selective. We will discuss diverse goals people seek explanations for, highlighting that effective explanations identify a difference maker, which is often causal. These discussions will lay the foundation for the rest of the tutorial.

We will then introduce the basic elements of explanations and their presentation, including explanation types and taxonomies, so that participants are familiar with the subject of evaluation. We will proceed with a taxonomy of human-centered evaluations, to include two primary types: application-grounded human-subjects evaluations and evaluations based on human-provided explanations.

We start with how to conduct *human-subjects studies* to evaluate explanations. We would like to encourage NLP researchers to move beyond using simplified evaluation tasks, to considering different usage scenarios of explantions and articulating evaluation goals—for whom and what purposes a given explanation method is meant to serve, then define the evaluation task, evaluation criteria, and

Proceedings of the 2022 Conference of the North American Chapter of the Association for Computational Linguistics Human Language Technologies: Tutorial Abstracts, pages 26 - 32
July 10-15, 2022 ©2022 Association for Computational Linguistics

recruiting requirement accordingly. We will also describe common methods to measure different evaluation criteria, such as survey scales and behavioral measurement, while raising limitations of existing methods.

Then, we cover evaluations with *evaluation based on human-annotated explanations*, as this area is more familiar with the NLP audience. This family of evaluations involves collecting explanations alongside ground-truth labels, and using these human-annotated explanations as a gold standard for model-generated explanations. While intuitive, this practice has validity issues associated with misalignment between human reasoning and model behavior, which we will discuss at length.

We will conclude the tutorial with a discussion of future directions for human-centered evaluation of explanations.

Flipped format. Our tutorial will be in a flipped format: participants view the videos asynchronously and participate in Q&A and work through hands-on activities. The flipped classroom has shown better retention than traditional instruction in a stand-alone instruction session (Bishop and Verleger, 2013). We believe the flipped format is also condusive for ACL tutorials: (1) it will have more longevity, as the recorded (and edited) videos will be of higher quality than videos recorded at a typical conference session; (2) it will be easier for hybrid participation; (3) it will be a more engaging experience for in-person participants.

All of the videos will be in segments of twenty minutes or less for easy asynchronous viewing. To ensure accessibility, we will have manual (not ASR) captions and distribute the slide source along with the videos for easier incorporation of the tutorial into classroom instruction.

Target Audience and Expected Pre-requisite. We welcome anyone who is interested in intepretable NLP and human-AI interaction and only require basic knowledge to programming and contemporary classification models.

2 Outline of the Tutorial Content and Reading List

The tutorial will consiste of two parts: (1) (offline) two hours of content to be viewed asynchronously and (2) (online or in-person) three hours of Q&A and hands-on activities. We include the cited references in the outline description.

2.1 Asynchronous Tutorial

Introduction. This section will introduce explainable AI (XAI) and the importance of evaluating explanations following a human-centered approach (i.e., evaluating with respect to stakeholder needs and desiredata).

Psychological foundation of explanations. This section will cover the research on human explanations in psychology that highlights the fact that human explanations are necessarily incomplete: we do not start from a set of axioms and present all the deductive steps. We will also explore the assumption on whether humans can provide explanations. Furthermore, to build the foundation for defining evaluation goals and criteria for model explanations, we will discuss the diverse goals people seek explanation for. Cited references: Aronowitz and Lombrozo (2020); Aslanov et al. (2021); Blanchard et al. (2018); Giffin et al. (2017); Wilson and Keil (1998); Hemmatian and Sloman (2018); Keil (2003); Kuhn (2001); Lipton (1990); Lombrozo (2012, 2016); Lombrozo et al. (2019); Woodward and Ross (2021).

Explanation methods. The design of evaluation studies is a primary focus of this tutorial. And the subject of these user studies is machine explanations. This section provides the necessary background knowledge on the generation and presentation of machine explanations. We will present a high-level taxonomy of explanation methods and the challenges each category presents to the evaluation. We cover both local explanations such as feature attribution (Ribeiro et al., 2016; Lundberg and Lee, 2017; Li et al., 2016) and counterfactuals (Goyal et al., 2019; Verma et al., 2020), and global explanations such as prototypes (Snell et al., 2017; Gurumoorthy et al., 2019) and adversarial rules (Ribeiro et al., 2018; Wallace et al., 2019). Our overview will omit technical details such as how to computate the input gradient for a specific neural network architecture. Instead, we will discuss the various design choices behind the presentation of explanations, such as color mapping, interactivity, and customizability. For example, local feature importance might be presented as highlighted words in a text classifier, whereas model uncertainty (or prediction probability) can be exposed as either a numerical value or pie chart. Explanations may be provided either alongside every prediction or only on demand. Explanations might be static information displays or interactive, supporting drilling in for more detail, questioning the system, or even providing feedback to improve it. We will also discuss the limitation of these explanation methods (Guo et al., 2017; Feng et al., 2018; Ye et al., 2021).

Evaluating explanations . We will then provide an overview of human-centered evaluation approaches.

AppliHuman-subjects evaluation . We will start by distinguishing between application-grounded evaluation, based on the success of target users' end goal, and simplified evaluation, such as asking people to simulate the model predictions based on its explanations (Doshi-Velez and Kim, 2017). While it is currently more common for NLP researchers to use simplified evaluation tasks, a recent HCI study pointed out their limitations and lack of evaluative power to predict the actual success in deployment (Buçinca et al., 2020). To encourage NLP researchers to move towards performing application-grounded evaluation, and in a principled and efficient fashion, we will introduce a taxonomy of common applications of explanations, user types and user goals (e.g., model diagnosis, decision improvement, trust calibration, auditing for biases) based on recent HCI work (Suresh et al., 2021; Liao et al., 2020). Using this framework, NLP researchers can articulate the user type(s) and user goal(s) that a given explanation method is meant to serve, and based on that define the evaluation tasks, criteria, subjects to recruit, and so on. We will cover common evaluation criteria regarding both the reception of explanations (e.g., easiness to understand, cognitive workload) and satisfaction of users' end goals, and discuss existing methods to measure them, such as survey scales and behavioral measures. We will also provide introductory contents on how to conduct human-subjects studies, such as how to recruit participants, design tasks and instructions, prevent data noises and biases, and common ethical concerns. We will also give case studies such as Dodge et al. (2019) and Lai and Tan (2019). This tutorial aims to promote important considerations in this nascent area and introduce existing methods from HCI to inspire establishing best practices. Additional references: (Liao and Varshney, 2021; Zhang et al., 2020; Wang and Yin, 2021; McKnight et al., 2002; Cheng et al., 2019; Lai et al., 2021; Kaur et al., 2020; Jacobs et al., 2020).

Evaluation based on human-provided explanations. We discuss the advantages and disadvantages of human-annotated explanations as a means for evaluating model explanations.

Numerous NLP datasets have been released with both labels and human-provided explanations. These come mostly in the form of *rationales* indicating which tokens within a text are important or causal for the true label, e.g., (Zaidan et al., 2007; Khashabi et al., 2018; Thorne et al., 2018), but sometimes consist of *natural language* e.g., (Camburu et al., 2018). DeYoung et al. (2019) aggregates several such datasets into one collection, while Wiegreffe and Marasović (2021) gives an overview of these datasets in the wider literature.

We discuss the metrics by which human-annotated explanations are used to evaluate model-generated explanations. This is a relatively straightforward sequence classification-style evaluation for rationale-type explanations (F1, MSE, etc.), but a more nuanced NLG-style evaluation for natural language explanations (Garbacea and Mei, 2020).

We conclude with a discussion of the validity of human-explanations as a gold standard for model explanations. Recent work has investigated the informational properties of human-annotated explanations, finding that there are gaps between what information humans believe is sufficient or necessary for prediction (i.e. human-annotated explanations), and what actually is so in practice for trained NLP models Carton et al. (2020); Hase et al. (2020). We discuss the implications of these analyses on the validity question, as well as on the future of this style of evaluation.

Summary and future directions . We will conclude by comparing these two main types of human-centered evaluations, recommending best practices, and discussing future directions.

2.2 Q&A and Tutorial Activities

For the in-person tutorial, we will provide a brief recap of the tutorial, followed by an interactive Q&A session and working group activities. We will choose two tasks based on pre-conference surveys as running examples, e.g., sentiment analysis and question answering. Please see the outline below.

- Recap (40 minutes).
- Q&A (40 minutes).

- Break (10 minutes).
- Activity 1: Get familiar with explanations (30 minutes). The main of this exercise is to get them to see how different explanation methods work in practice. We will provide a notebook and models to be used.
- Activity 2: Hands-on participatory evaluation (60 minutes). We will have two tracks that are aligned with the two approaches, one for explanation dataset collection, one for human subject evaluation. It has two steps: 1) research design and 2) participatory evaluation. In this first step, we will ask people to either come up with annotation guideline or articulate evaluation goals (e.g., what user goal(s) and user type(s) is it meant to serve) and define evaluation criteria (e.g., evaluation tasks and measurements). In the second step, parcipants will exchange and participate in the study designed in the first step by either annotating explanations based on the guidelines or performing user studies based on the tasks.

3 Expected Outcome

We plan to make tutorial presentation materials public. We will make sure the videos are accessible to a wide population, e.g., via transcripts.

Estimated audience size. We estimate that ~200 people will attend the tutorial. The algorithmic counterpart, Wallace et al. (2020), was one of the most popular tutorials at EMNLP that year.

4 Diversity Considerations

Our speakers are diverse in discipline (NLP, HCI, and psychology), gender (4 male, 3 female), seniority (from professor to postdocs), academia and industry (5 from acadmia, 2 from industry).

Our flipped format will accomodate a diverse group of audience because of its asychronous nature. For example, non-native speakers have more time to digest the content. We also require a low barrier of entry. To further attract a diverse group of participants, we will advertise this through underrepresented groups such as Women in NLP, Black in AI, and Queer in AI.

5 Presenter Biographies

Jordan Boyd-Graber is an associate professor at the University of Maryland, with joint appointments between computer science, the iSchool, language science, and the Institute for Advanced Computer Studies. He has been teaching using a flipped classroom approach since 2013. He and his collaborators helped end the use of perplexity for topic models (Chang et al., 2009), first developed interactive topic models (Hu et al., 2011), and improved word-level analysis of topic model explanations (Lund et al., 2019). Additional information at: `http://boydgraber.org`.

Samuel Carton is a postdoctoral researcher at the University of Colorado, Boulder. His interests lie in model interpretability and human-AI interaction. Additional information at: `https://shcarton.github.io`.

Shi Feng is a postdoctoral researcher at the Uhiversity of Chicago. His research interests include interpretable NLP, adversarial robustness, and alignment. Additional information at: `http://www.shifeng.umiacs.io/`.

Q. Vera Liao is a Principal Researcher at Microsoft Research Montreal, where she is part of the FATE (Fairness, Accountability, Transparency, and Ethics) group. She is an HCI researcher by training, with current interest in human-AI interaction and explainable AI. More information can be found at: `http://www.qveraliao.com/`

Tania Lombrozo is the Arthur W. Marks '19 Professor of Psychology at Princeton University. She is a leading expert in understanding explanations. Additional information is available at: `http://cognition.princeton.edu/`.

Alison Smith-Renner is a Senior Research Scientist in human-AI interaction at Dataminr. Her research interests include explainable and interactive natural language processing from a human-centric perspective. Additional information is available at: `https://alisonmsmith.github.io`

Chenhao Tan is an assistant professor of computer science at the University of Chicago, and is also affiliated with the Harris School of Public Policy. His research interest includes natural language processing, human-centered AI, and computational social science. Additional information is available at: `https://chenhaot.com`

6 Technical Requirements

For the in-person tutorial, we request roundtables so that participants can discuss together during the Q&A and the workshop activities; it would be good to have power outlets around the tables.

7 Ethics Statement

Our tutorial takes a human-centered perspective. We hope that our tutorial will broaden the scope of evaluations in NLP by introducing perspectives from HCI and psychology. This may help alleviate ethical concerns of NLP models in the long run by incorporating human perspectives into the development and evaluation process.

8 Special Themes

Our tutorial is alighed with the special theme of NAACL 2022, human-centered natural language processing.

References

Sara Aronowitz and Tania Lombrozo. 2020. Experiential explanation. *Topics in Cognitive Science*, 12(4):1321–1336.

Ivan A Aslanov, Yulia V Sudorgina, and Alexey A Kotov. 2021. The explanatory effect of a label: Its influence on a category persists even if we forget the label. *Frontiers in Psychology*, 12:745586–745586.

Jacob Bishop and Matthew A Verleger. 2013. The flipped classroom: A survey of the research. In *2013 ASEE Annual Conference & Exposition*, 10.18260/1-2–22585, Atlanta, Georgia. ASEE Conferences. Https://peer.asee.org/22585.

Thomas Blanchard, Nadya Vasilyeva, and Tania Lombrozo. 2018. Stability, breadth and guidance. *Philosophical Studies*, 175(9):2263–2283.

Zana Buçinca, Phoebe Lin, Krzysztof Z Gajos, and Elena L Glassman. 2020. Proxy tasks and subjective measures can be misleading in evaluating explainable ai systems. In *Proceedings of the 25th International Conference on Intelligent User Interfaces*, pages 454–464.

Oana-Maria Camburu, Tim Rocktäschel, Thomas Lukasiewicz, and Phil Blunsom. 2018. e-SNLI: Natural Language Inference with Natural Language Explanations. In S. Bengio, H. Wallach, H. Larochelle, K. Grauman, N. Cesa-Bianchi, and R. Garnett, editors, *Advances in Neural Information Processing Systems 31*, pages 9539–9549. Curran Associates, Inc.

Samuel Carton, Anirudh Rathore, and Chenhao Tan. 2020. Evaluating and Characterizing Human Rationales. In *Proceedings of the 2020 Conference on Empirical Methods in Natural Language Processing (EMNLP)*, pages 9294–9307, Online. Association for Computational Linguistics.

Jonathan Chang, Jordan Boyd-Graber, Chong Wang, Sean Gerrish, and David M. Blei. 2009. Reading tea leaves: How humans interpret topic models. In *Proceedings of Advances in Neural Information Processing Systems*.

Hao-Fei Cheng, Ruotong Wang, Zheng Zhang, Fiona O'Connell, Terrance Gray, F Maxwell Harper, and Haiyi Zhu. 2019. Explaining decision-making algorithms through ui: Strategies to help non-expert stakeholders. In *Proceedings of the 2019 chi conference on human factors in computing systems*, pages 1–12.

Jay DeYoung, Sarthak Jain, Nazneen Fatema Rajani, Eric Lehman, Caiming Xiong, Richard Socher, and Byron C. Wallace. 2019. ERASER: A Benchmark to Evaluate Rationalized NLP Models. *arXiv preprint*. ArXiv: 1911.03429.

Jonathan Dodge, Q Vera Liao, Yunfeng Zhang, Rachel KE Bellamy, and Casey Dugan. 2019. Explaining models: an empirical study of how explanations impact fairness judgment. In *Proceedings of the 24th international conference on intelligent user interfaces*, pages 275–285.

Finale Doshi-Velez and Been Kim. 2017. Towards a rigorous science of interpretable machine learning. *arXiv preprint arXiv:1702.08608*.

Shi Feng, Eric Wallace, Alvin Grissom II, Mohit Iyyer, Pedro Rodriguez, and Jordan Boyd-Graber. 2018. Pathologies of neural models make interpretations difficult.

Cristina Garbacea and Qiaozhu Mei. 2020. Neural Language Generation: Formulation, Methods, and Evaluation. *arXiv:2007.15780 [cs]*. ArXiv: 2007.15780.

Carly Giffin, Daniel Wilkenfeld, and Tania Lombrozo. 2017. The explanatory effect of a label: Explanations with named categories are more satisfying. *Cognition*, 168:357–369.

Yash Goyal, Ziyan Wu, Jan Ernst, Dhruv Batra, Devi Parikh, and Stefan Lee. 2019. Counterfactual visual explanations. In *International Conference on Machine Learning*, pages 2376–2384. PMLR.

Chuan Guo, Geoff Pleiss, Yu Sun, and Kilian Q Weinberger. 2017. On calibration of modern neural networks. In *International Conference on Machine Learning*, pages 1321–1330. PMLR.

Karthik S Gurumoorthy, Amit Dhurandhar, Guillermo Cecchi, and Charu Aggarwal. 2019. Efficient data representation by selecting prototypes with importance weights. In *2019 IEEE International Conference on Data Mining (ICDM)*, pages 260–269. IEEE.

Peter Hase, Shiyue Zhang, Harry Xie, and Mohit Bansal. 2020. Leakage-Adjusted Simulatability: Can Models Generate Non-Trivial Explanations of Their Behavior in Natural Language? *arXiv:2010.04119 [cs]*. ArXiv: 2010.04119.

Babak Hemmatian and Steven A Sloman. 2018. Community appeal: Explanation without information. *Journal of Experimental Psychology: General*, 147(11):1677.

Yuening Hu, Jordan Boyd-Graber, and Brianna Satinoff. 2011. Interactive topic modeling. In *Proceedings of the Association for Computational Linguistics*.

Abigail Z Jacobs, Su Lin Blodgett, Solon Barocas, Hal Daumé III, and Hanna Wallach. 2020. The meaning and measurement of bias: lessons from natural language processing. In *Proceedings of the 2020 Conference on Fairness, Accountability, and Transparency*, pages 706–706.

Harmanpreet Kaur, Harsha Nori, Samuel Jenkins, Rich Caruana, Hanna Wallach, and Jennifer Wortman Vaughan. 2020. Interpreting interpretability: understanding data scientists' use of interpretability tools for machine learning. In *Proceedings of the 2020 CHI conference on human factors in computing systems*, pages 1–14.

Frank C Keil. 2003. Folkscience: Coarse interpretations of a complex reality. *Trends in cognitive sciences*, 7(8):368–373.

Daniel Khashabi, Snigdha Chaturvedi, Michael Roth, Shyam Upadhyay, and Dan Roth. 2018. Looking Beyond the Surface: A Challenge Set for Reading Comprehension over Multiple Sentences. In *Proceedings of the 2018 Conference of the North American Chapter of the Association for Computational Linguistics: Human Language Technologies, Volume 1 (Long Papers)*, pages 252–262, New Orleans, Louisiana. Association for Computational Linguistics.

Deanna Kuhn. 2001. How do people know? *Psychological science*, 12(1):1–8.

Vivian Lai, Chacha Chen, Q Vera Liao, Alison Smith-Renner, and Chenhao Tan. 2021. Towards a science of human-ai decision making: A survey of empirical studies. *arXiv preprint arXiv:2112.11471*.

Vivian Lai and Chenhao Tan. 2019. On human predictions with explanations and predictions of machine learning models: A case study on deception detection. In *Proceedings of FAT**.

Jiwei Li, Will Monroe, and Dan Jurafsky. 2016. Understanding neural networks through representation erasure. *arXiv preprint arXiv:1612.08220*.

Q Vera Liao, Daniel Gruen, and Sarah Miller. 2020. Questioning the ai: informing design practices for explainable ai user experiences. In *Proceedings of the 2020 CHI Conference on Human Factors in Computing Systems*, pages 1–15.

Q Vera Liao and Kush R Varshney. 2021. Human-centered explainable ai (xai): From algorithms to user experiences. *arXiv preprint arXiv:2110.10790*.

Peter Lipton. 1990. Contrastive explanation. *Royal Institute of Philosophy Supplements*, 27:247–266.

Tania Lombrozo. 2012. Explanation and abductive inference.

Tania Lombrozo. 2016. Explanatory preferences shape learning and inference. *Trends in Cognitive Sciences*, 20(10):748–759.

Tania Lombrozo, Daniel Wilkenfeld, T Lombrozo, and D Wilkenfeld. 2019. Mechanistic versus functional understanding. *Varieties of understanding: New perspectives from philosophy, psychology, and theology*, pages 209–229.

Jeffrey Lund, Piper Armstrong, Wilson Fearn, Stephen Cowley, Courtni Byun, Jordan Boyd-Graber, and Kevin Seppi. 2019. Automatic and human evaluation of local topic quality. In *Association for Computational Linguistics*.

Scott M Lundberg and Su-In Lee. 2017. A unified approach to interpreting model predictions. In *Proceedings of the 31st international conference on neural information processing systems*, pages 4768–4777.

D Harrison McKnight, Vivek Choudhury, and Charles Kacmar. 2002. Developing and validating trust measures for e-commerce: An integrative typology. *Information systems research*, 13(3):334–359.

Marco Tulio Ribeiro, Sameer Singh, and Carlos Guestrin. 2016. "why should i trust you?" explaining the predictions of any classifier. In *Proceedings of the 22nd ACM SIGKDD international conference on knowledge discovery and data mining*, pages 1135–1144.

Marco Tulio Ribeiro, Sameer Singh, and Carlos Guestrin. 2018. Semantically equivalent adversarial rules for debugging nlp models. In *Proceedings of the 56th Annual Meeting of the Association for Computational Linguistics (Volume 1: Long Papers)*, pages 856–865.

Jake Snell, Kevin Swersky, and Richard S Zemel. 2017. Prototypical networks for few-shot learning. *arXiv preprint arXiv:1703.05175*.

Harini Suresh, Steven R Gomez, Kevin K Nam, and Arvind Satyanarayan. 2021. Beyond expertise and roles: A framework to characterize the stakeholders of interpretable machine learning and their needs. In *Proceedings of the 2021 CHI Conference on Human Factors in Computing Systems*, pages 1–16.

James Thorne, Andreas Vlachos, Christos Christodoulopoulos, and Arpit Mittal. 2018. FEVER: a large-scale dataset for Fact Extraction and VERification. *arXiv:1803.05355 [cs]*. ArXiv: 1803.05355.

Sahil Verma, John Dickerson, and Keegan Hines. 2020. Counterfactual explanations for machine learning: A review. *arXiv preprint arXiv:2010.10596*.

Eric Wallace, Shi Feng, Nikhil Kandpal, Matt Gardner, and Sameer Singh. 2019. Universal adversarial triggers for attacking and analyzing nlp. *arXiv preprint arXiv:1908.07125*.

Eric Wallace, Matt Gardner, and Sameer Singh. 2020. Interpreting predictions of NLP models. In *Proceedings of the 2020 Conference on Empirical Methods in Natural Language Processing: Tutorial Abstracts*, pages 20–23, Online. Association for Computational Linguistics.

Xinru Wang and Ming Yin. 2021. Are explanations helpful? a comparative study of the effects of explanations in ai-assisted decision-making. In *26th International Conference on Intelligent User Interfaces*, pages 318–328.

Sarah Wiegreffe and Ana Marasović. 2021. Teach Me to Explain: A Review of Datasets for Explainable NLP. *arXiv:2102.12060 [cs]*. ArXiv: 2102.12060.

Robert A Wilson and Frank Keil. 1998. The shadows and shallows of explanation. *Minds and machines*, 8(1):137–159.

James Woodward and Lauren Ross. 2021. Scientific Explanation. In Edward N. Zalta, editor, *The Stanford Encyclopedia of Philosophy*, Summer 2021 edition. Metaphysics Research Lab, Stanford University.

Xi Ye, Rohan Nair, and Greg Durrett. 2021. Connecting attributions and qa model behavior on realistic counterfactuals. *arXiv preprint arXiv:2104.04515*.

Omar Zaidan, Jason Eisner, and Christine Piatko. 2007. Using "Annotator Rationales" to Improve Machine Learning for Text Categorization. In *Human Language Technologies 2007: The Conference of the North American Chapter of the Association for Computational Linguistics; Proceedings of the Main Conference*, pages 260–267, Rochester, New York. Association for Computational Linguistics.

Yunfeng Zhang, Q Vera Liao, and Rachel KE Bellamy. 2020. Effect of confidence and explanation on accuracy and trust calibration in ai-assisted decision making. In *Proceedings of the 2020 Conference on Fairness, Accountability, and Transparency*, pages 295–305.

Tutorial on Multimodal Machine Learning

Louis-Philippe Morency, Paul Pu Liang, Amir Zadeh
Carnegie Mellon University
{morency,pliang,abagherz}@cs.cmu.edu
https://cmu-multicomp-lab.github.io/mmml-tutorial/naacl2022/

Abstract

Multimodal machine learning involves integrating and modeling information from multiple heterogeneous and interconnected sources of data. It is a challenging yet crucial area with numerous real-world applications in multimedia, affective computing, robotics, finance, HCI, and healthcare. This tutorial, building upon a new edition of a survey paper on multimodal ML as well as previously-given tutorials and academic courses, will describe an updated taxonomy on multimodal machine learning synthesizing its core technical challenges and major directions for future research.

1 Introduction

Multimodal machine learning is a vibrant multi-disciplinary research field that addresses some original goals of AI by integrating and modeling multiple communicative modalities, including linguistic, acoustic, and visual messages. With the initial research on audio-visual speech recognition and more recently with language & vision projects such as image and video captioning, visual question answering, and language-guided reinforcement learning, this research field brings some unique challenges for multimodal researchers given the heterogeneity of the data and the contingency often found between modalities.

This tutorial builds upon the annual course on Multimodal Machine Learning taught at Carnegie Mellon University and is a revised version of the previous tutorials on multimodal learning at CVPR 2021, ACL 2017, CVPR 2016, and ICMI 2016. These previous tutorials were based on our earlier survey on multimodal machine learning, which introduced an initial taxonomy for core multimodal challenges (Baltrusaitis et al., 2019). The present tutorial is based on a revamped taxonomy of the core technical challenges and updated concepts about recent work in multimodal machine learning (Liang et al., 2022). The tutorial will be centered around six core challenges in multimodal machine learning:

1. Representation: A first fundamental challenge is to learn representations that exploit cross-modal interactions between individual elements of different modalities. The heterogeneity of multimodal data makes it particularly challenging to learn multimodal representations. We will cover fundamental approaches for (1) *representation fusion* (integrating information from 2 or more modalities, effectively reducing the number of separate representations), (2) *representation coordination* (interchanging cross-modal information with the goal of keeping the same number of representations but improving multimodal contextualization), and (3) *representation fission* (creating a new disjoint set of representations, usually larger number than the input set, that reflects knowledge about internal structure such as data clustering or factorization).

2. Alignment: A second challenge is to identify the connections between all elements of different modalities using their structure and cross-modal interactions. For example, when analyzing the speech and gestures of a human subject, how can we align specific gestures with spoken words or utterances? Alignment between modalities is challenging since it may exist at different (1) *granularities* (words, utterances, frames, videos), involve varying (2) *correspondences* (one-to-one, many-to-many, or not exist at all), and depend on long-range (3) *dependencies*.

3. Reasoning is defined as composing knowledge from multimodal evidences, usually through multiple inferential steps, to exploit multimodal alignment and problem structure for a specific task. This relationship often follows some hierarchical structure, where more abstract concepts are defined higher in the hierarchy as a function of less abstract concepts. Multimodal reasoning involves the subchallenges of capturing this (1) *structure* (through domain knowledge or discovered from

Proceedings of the 2022 Conference of the North American Chapter of the Association for Computational Linguistics Human Language Technologies: Tutorial Abstracts, pages 33 - 38

data), the parameterization of (2) *concepts* (dense vs interpretable and symbolic), and the type of (3) *composition* (simple vs complex relationships).

4. Generation: The fourth challenge involves learning a generative process to produce raw modalities that reflect cross-modal interactions, structure and coherence. We categorize its subchallenges into (1) *summarization* (summarizing multimodal data to reduce information content while highlighting the most salient parts of the input), (2) *translation* (translating from one modality to another and keeping information content while being consistent with cross-modal interactions), and (3) *creation* (simultaneously generating multiple modalities to increase information content while maintaining coherence within and across modalities). We will also cover advances in evaluation and ethical concerns around generated content.

5. Transference: A fifth challenge is to transfer knowledge between modalities and their representations, usually to help the target modality, which may be noisy or with limited resources. Exemplified by algorithms of (1) *transfer* (fine-tuning pre-trained models for a downstream task involving the target modality), (2) *representation enrichment* (transfer through a joint model sharing representation spaces between both modalities), and (3) *model induction* (keeping individual unimodal models separate but transferring information across these models), how can knowledge learned from one modality (e.g., predicted labels or representation) help a computational model trained on a different modality?

6. Quantification involves a deeper measurement and theoretical study of multimodal models to better understand their (1) *output qualities* (the extent to which models are predictive, efficient, and robust under natural and targeted modality imperfections), (2) *internal mechanics* (understanding the internal modeling of multimodal information and cross-modal interactions), and (3) *modality tradeoffs* (quantifying the utility and risks of each input modality, while balancing these tradeoffs for reliable real-world usage). It is important to obtain a deeper understanding of the data, modeling, and optimization challenges involved when learning from heterogeneous data in order to improve their robustness, interpretability, and reliability in real-world multimodal applications.

Type of tutorial: This tutorial will begin with basic concepts related to multimodal research before describing cutting-edge research in the context of the six core challenges.

Target audience and expected background: We expect the audience to have an introductory background in machine learning and deep learning, including a basic familiarity of commonly-used unimodal building blocks such as convolutional, recurrent, and self-attention models.

2 Tutorial outline

This tutorial will be a revised edition of our previously-organized tutorials at CVPR 2022, CVPR 2021, ACL 2017, CVPR 2016, and ICMI 2016 which were roughly 3-4 hours long. This revision defines a new iteration of the taxonomy that has been updated to help researchers tackle modern multimodal challenges. The tutorial outline is shown below:

Introduction (30 mins)

- What is Multimodal? Definitions, dimensions of heterogeneity and cross-modal interactions.
- Historical view and multimodal research tasks.
- Core technical challenges: representation, alignment, transference, reasoning, generation, and quantification.
- Unimodal language, visual, and acoustic representations.

Representation (30 mins)

- Representation fusion: fusion strategies, multimodal auto-encoder.
- Representation coordination: contrastive learning, vector-space models, canonical correlation analysis.
- Representation fission: factorization, component analysis, disentanglement.

===== BREAK =====

Alignment (25 mins)

- Granularity: segmentation, clustering, unit definition.

- Correspondences: latent alignment approaches, attention models, multimodal transformers, multi-instance learning.

- Dependency types: Attention models, graph neural networks, multimodal transformers, multi-instance learning.

Transference (25 mins)

- Modality transfer: losses, hallucination, cross-modal transfer.

- Foundation models: pre-trained models and adaptation.

- Model induction: co-training, cross-modal learning.

===== BREAK =====

Reasoning (20 mins)

- Structure: hierarchical, graphical, temporal, and interactive structure, structure discovery.

- Concepts: dense and neuro-symbolic.

- Composition: causal and logical relationships.

- Knowledge: external knowledge bases, commonsense reasoning.

Generation (15 mins)

- Summarization, translation, and creation.

- Model evaluation and ethical concerns.

Quantification (25 mins)

- Output qualities: generalization, robustness, complexity.

- Internal mechanics: interpretability, understanding cross-model interactions.

- Modality tradeoffs: dataset biases, social biases, theoretical benefits, optimization challenges.

Future directions and conclusion (10 mins)

3 Tutorial details

Included work: The tutorial is based on an updated version (Liang et al., 2022) of the broadly cited survey on multimodal ML (Baltrusaitis et al., 2019) which covers fundamental work in multimodal, including affective computing (Poria et al., 2017), audio-visual learning, image and video-based question answering (Agrawal et al., 2017), media description (Vinyals et al., 2016), multimodal machine translation (Yao and Wan, 2020), multimodal reinforcement learning (Luketina et al., 2019), and social impacts of real-world multimodal learning (Liang et al., 2021). The updated survey will be released with this tutorial, following the six core challenges mentioned earlier. While the taxonomy is developed by the organizers, most of the presented work comes from the broader research community.

Diversity: This tutorial will cover multilingual tasks (e.g. multimodal machine translation) and multiple research domains (image, text, audio). This tutorial brings together faculty, graduate students, and postdoctoral researchers. Slides will also be dedicated to low-data language and modality scenarios.

Reading list: We suggest the following reading list. These papers can be skimmed through before the tutorial, and are also well-served as reading material for after the tutorial. A more comprehensive reading list can be found in the multimodal ML courses at CMU, see `https://cmu-multicomp-lab.github.io/adv-mmml-course/spring2022/` and `https://cmu-multicomp-lab.github.io/mmml-course/fall2020/` for more details.

1. General: Fundamentals of Multimodal Machine Learning: A Taxonomy and Open Challenges (Liang et al., 2022)

2. General: Multimodal Machine Learning: A Survey and Taxonomy (Baltrusaitis et al., 2019)

3. General: Representation learning: A review and new perspectives (Bengio et al., 2013)

4. Representation: Multiplicative Interactions and Where to Find Them (Jayakumar et al., 2020)

5. Representation: Multimodal Learning with Deep Boltzmann Machines (Srivastava and Salakhutdinov, 2014)

6. Representation: Learning Factorized Multimodal Representations (Tsai et al., 2019)

7. Alignment: Decoupling the Role of Data, Attention, and Losses in Multimodal Transformers (Hendricks et al., 2021)

8. Alignment: Deep canonical correlation analysis (Andrew et al., 2013)

9. Transference: Vokenization: Improving Language Understanding via Contextualized, Visually-Grounded Supervision (Tan and Bansal, 2020)

10. Transference: Foundations of Multimodal Co-learning (Zadeh et al., 2020)

11. Reasoning: The Neuro-Symbolic Concept Learner: Interpreting Scenes, Words, and Sentences From Natural Supervision (Mao et al., 2018)

12. Reasoning: A Survey of Reinforcement Learning Informed by Natural Language (Luketina et al., 2019)

13. Reasoning: VQA-LOL: Visual Question Answering Under the Lens of Logic (Gokhale et al., 2020)

14. Generation: Cross-modal Coherence Modeling for Caption Generation (Alikhani et al., 2020)

15. Generation: Zero-shot Text-to-Image Generation (Ramesh et al., 2021)

16. Quantification: MultiBench: Multiscale Benchmarks for Multimodal Representation Learning (Liang et al., 2021)

17. Quantification: M2Lens: Visualizing and Explaining Multimodal Models for Sentiment Analysis (Wang et al., 2021)

18. Quantification: Women also Snowboard: Overcoming Bias in Captioning Models (Hendricks et al., 2018)

4 Organizers

Louis-Philippe Morency (LTI, CMU) is an Associate Professor at CMU Language Technology Institute where he leads the Multimodal Communication and Machine Learning Laboratory (MultiComp Lab). He received his Ph.D. and Master's degrees from MIT Computer Science and Artificial Intelligence Laboratory. In 2008, Dr. Morency was selected as one of "AI's 10 to Watch" by IEEE Intelligent Systems. He has received 7 best paper awards in multiple ACM- and IEEE-sponsored conferences for his work on context-based gesture recognition, multimodal probabilistic fusion, and computational models of human communication dynamics. He has taught 10 editions of the multimodal machine learning course at CMU and before that at the University of Southern California. He has given multiple tutorials on this topic, including at ACL 2017, CVPR 2016, and ICMI 2016.

Paul Pu Liang (MLD, CMU) is a Ph.D. student in Machine Learning at Carnegie Mellon University, advised by Louis-Philippe Morency and Ruslan Salakhutdinov. His research is centered around building socially intelligent embodied agents with the ability to perceive and engage in multimodal human communication. He was a recipient of the distinguished student paper award at the NeurIPS 2019 workshop on federated learning and the best paper honorable mention award at ICMI 2017. He organized the workshop on human multimodal language at ACL 2020 and ACL 2018, the workshop on tensor networks at NeurIPS 2020, and was a workflow chair for ICML 2019.

Amir Zadeh (LTI, CMU) is a Postdoctoral Associate at Carnegie Mellon University. Prior to that, he received his Ph.D. from Language Technologies Institute, School of Computer Science, Carnegie Mellon University. His work is focused on multimodal learning, especially modeling multimodal language. He is the creator of several resources in this area including CMU-MOSEAS, CMU-MOSEI, and CMU-MOSI datasets. He organized the 1st and 2nd Workshop and Grand-Challenge on Multimodal Language in ACL 2018 and ACL 2020 respectively. His work has been published in ACL, EMNLP, NAACL, CVPR, and ICLR conferences.

5 Logistics

Audience size and previous editions: Our tutorial build upon 5 previous tutorials:

- CVPR 2022: 100-150 attendees. 6-hour tutorial `https://cmu-multicomp-lab.github.io/mmml-tutorial/cvpr2022/`
- CVPR 2021: 100-150 attendees. 6-hour tutorial `https://audio-visual-scene-understanding.github.io/`
- ACL 2017: 100-150 attendees. 4-hour tutorial (Morency and Baltrušaitis, 2017)
- CVPR 2016: 150-200 attendees. 4-hour tutorial: `https://sites.google.com/site/multiml2016cvpr/`
- ICMI 2016: 50-60 attendees, 3-hour tutorial: `https://icmi.acm.org/2016/index.php?id=tutorial`

This tutorial builds upon the annual Multimodal Machine Learning course taught at CMU (course 11-877 and 11-777). For recent iterations of the course, the materials are publicly available at:

- `https://cmu-multicomp-lab.github.io/adv-mmml-course/spring2022/`
- `https://cmu-multicomp-lab.github.io/mmml-course/fall2020/`
- `https://piazza.com/cmu/fall2019/11777/resources`

In Fall 2020, the course was virtual and all lecture videos were recorded and publicly available on YouTube. These videos have become hugely popular, amassing close to $50,000$ views.

Ethics statement: Multimodal models used in real-world applications can pose several considerations such as having higher time and space complexity as compared to unimodal tasks, privacy and security resulting from human-centric multimodal data, and capturing social biases through human language, human faces, human audio, and other multimodal data sources. Our tutorial will cover these risks of multimodal learning and describe recent work towards addressing these critical issues.

References

Aishwarya Agrawal, Jiasen Lu, Stanislaw Antol, Margaret Mitchell, C. Lawrence Zitnick, Devi Parikh, and Dhruv Batra. 2017. VQA: Visual question answering. *International Journal of Computer Vision*.

Malihe Alikhani, Piyush Sharma, Shengjie Li, Radu Soricut, and Matthew Stone. 2020. Cross-modal coherence modeling for caption generation. In *Proceedings of the 58th Annual Meeting of the Association for Computational Linguistics*, pages 6525–6535.

Galen Andrew, Raman Arora, Jeff Bilmes, and Karen Livescu. 2013. Deep canonical correlation analysis. In *International conference on machine learning*, pages 1247–1255. PMLR.

Tadas Baltrusaitis, Chaitanya Ahuja, and Louis-Philippe Morency. 2019. Multimodal machine learning: A survey and taxonomy. *IEEE Trans. Pattern Anal. Mach. Intell.*, 41(2):423–443.

Yoshua Bengio, Aaron Courville, and Pascal Vincent. 2013. Representation learning: A review and new perspectives. *IEEE transactions on pattern analysis and machine intelligence*, 35(8):1798–1828.

Tejas Gokhale, Pratyay Banerjee, Chitta Baral, and Yezhou Yang. 2020. Vqa-lol: Visual question answering under the lens of logic. In *European conference on computer vision*, pages 379–396. Springer.

Lisa Anne Hendricks, Kaylee Burns, Kate Saenko, Trevor Darrell, and Anna Rohrbach. 2018. Women also snowboard: Overcoming bias in captioning models. In *Proceedings of the European Conference on Computer Vision (ECCV)*, pages 771–787.

Lisa Anne Hendricks, John Mellor, Rosalia Schneider, Jean-Baptiste Alayrac, and Aida Nematzadeh. 2021. Decoupling the role of data, attention, and losses in multimodal transformers. *Transactions of the Association for Computational Linguistics*.

Siddhant M. Jayakumar, Wojciech M. Czarnecki, Jacob Menick, Jonathan Schwarz, Jack Rae, Simon Osindero, Yee Whye Teh, Tim Harley, and Razvan Pascanu. 2020. Multiplicative interactions and where to find them. In *International Conference on Learning Representations*.

Paul Pu Liang, Yiwei Lyu, Xiang Fan, Zetian Wu, Yun Cheng, Jason Wu, Leslie Yufan Chen, Peter Wu, Michelle A Lee, Yuke Zhu, Ruslan Salakhutdinov, and Louis-Philippe Morency. 2021. Multibench: Multiscale benchmarks for multimodal representation learning. In *NeurIPS Datasets and Benchmarks Track*.

Paul Pu Liang, Amir Zadeh, and Louis-Philippe Morency. 2022. Foundations of multimodal machine learning: A taxonomy and open challenges. *arXiv preprint*.

Jelena Luketina, Nantas Nardelli, Gregory Farquhar, Jakob N Foerster, Jacob Andreas, Edward Grefenstette, Shimon Whiteson, and Tim Rocktäschel. 2019. A survey of reinforcement learning informed by natural language. In *IJCAI*.

Jiayuan Mao, Chuang Gan, Pushmeet Kohli, Joshua B Tenenbaum, and Jiajun Wu. 2018. The neuro-symbolic concept learner: Interpreting scenes, words, and sentences from natural supervision. In *International Conference on Learning Representations*.

Louis-Philippe Morency and Tadas Baltrušaitis. 2017. Multimodal machine learning: Integrating language, vision and speech. In *Proceedings of the 55th Annual Meeting of the Association for Computational Linguistics: Tutorial Abstracts*, pages 3–5, Vancouver, Canada. Association for Computational Linguistics.

Soujanya Poria, Erik Cambria, Rajiv Bajpai, and Amir Hussain. 2017. A review of affective computing: From unimodal analysis to multimodal fusion. *Information Fusion*.

Aditya Ramesh, Mikhail Pavlov, Gabriel Goh, Scott Gray, Chelsea Voss, Alec Radford, Mark Chen, and Ilya Sutskever. 2021. Zero-shot text-to-image generation. In *International Conference on Machine Learning*, pages 8821–8831. PMLR.

Nitish Srivastava and Ruslan Salakhutdinov. 2014. Multimodal learning with deep boltzmann machines. *J. Mach. Learn. Res.*, 15(1):2949–2980.

Hao Tan and Mohit Bansal. 2020. Vokenization: Improving language understanding via contextualized, visually-grounded supervision. In *Proceedings of the 2020 Conference on Empirical Methods in Natural Language Processing (EMNLP)*, pages 2066–2080.

Yao-Hung Hubert Tsai, Paul Pu Liang, Amir Zadeh, Louis-Philippe Morency, and Ruslan Salakhutdinov. 2019. Learning factorized multimodal representations. *ICLR*.

Oriol Vinyals, Alexander Toshev, Samy Bengio, and Dumitru Erhan. 2016. Show and tell: Lessons learned from the 2015 mscoco image captioning challenge. *IEEE transactions on pattern analysis and machine intelligence*, 39(4):652–663.

Xingbo Wang, Jianben He, Zhihua Jin, Muqiao Yang, Yong Wang, and Huamin Qu. 2021. M2lens: visualizing and explaining multimodal models for sentiment analysis. *IEEE Transactions on Visualization and Computer Graphics*, 28(1):802–812.

Shaowei Yao and Xiaojun Wan. 2020. Multimodal transformer for multimodal machine translation. In *Proceedings of the 58th Annual Meeting of the Association for Computational Linguistics*, Online. Association for Computational Linguistics.

Amir Zadeh, Paul Pu Liang, and Louis-Philippe Morency. 2020. Foundations of multimodal co-learning. *Information Fusion*, 64:188–193.

Contrastive Data and Learning for Natural Language Processing

Rui Zhang
Penn State University
rmz5227@psu.edu

Yangfeng Ji
University of Virginia
yangfeng@virginia.edu

Yue Zhang
Westlake University
yue.zhang@wias.org.cn

Rebecca J. Passonneau
Penn State University
rjp49@psu.edu

1 Brief Description

Current NLP models heavily rely on effective representation learning algorithms. Contrastive learning is one such technique to learn an embedding space such that similar data sample pairs have close representations while dissimilar samples stay far apart from each other. It can be used in supervised or unsupervised settings using different loss functions to produce task-specific or general-purpose representations. While it has originally enabled the success for vision tasks, recent years have seen a growing number of publications in contrastive NLP as shown in Figure 1. This first line of works not only delivers promising performance improvements in various NLP tasks, but also provides desired characteristics such as task-agnostic sentence representation, faithful text generation, data-efficient learning in zero-shot and few-shot settings, interpretability and explainability.

In this tutorial, we aim to provide a gentle introduction to the fundamentals of contrastive learning approaches and the theory behind them. We then survey the benefits and the best practices of contrastive learning for various downstream NLP applications including Text Classification, Question Answering, Summarization, Text Generation, Interpretability and Explainability, Commonsense Knowledge and Reasoning, Vision-and-Language. This tutorial intends to help researchers in the NLP and computational linguistics community to understand this emerging topic and promote future research directions of using contrastive learning for NLP applications.[1]

Type of Tutorial: Cutting-edge As an emerging approach, recent years have seen a growing number of NLP papers using contrastive learning (Figure 1). Contrastive learning still has a huge potential in other applications and challenges, and

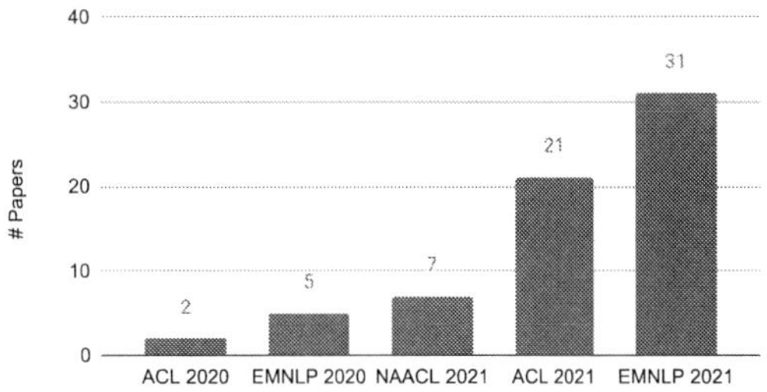

Figure 1: The number of papers in recent *ACL conferences with "contrastive learning" in the title. We anticipate there will be even more papers in 2022.

we anticipate there will be even more papers in the next year before this tutorial. However, there is no tutorial yet that systematically introduces contrastive learning and its application to NLP.

Target Audience and Expected Background This tutorial is targeted at a broad and general audience who is interested using contrastive learning for NLP tasks. The tutorial will be self-contained. The expected prerequisite only includes basic a understanding of machine learning concepts such as classification, loss functions, and gradient-based optimization. We also expect the audience to be familiar with the definition of different NLP tasks.

2 Tutorial Structure and Content

This tutorial first gives an introduction to the foundation of contrastive learning and then reviews the NLP application of contrastive learning. Our tutorial covers both **contrastive data augmentation for NLP** and **contrastive representation learning for NLP**. The former focuses on the data side: how we can create contrastive data examples. This is useful not only for contrastive learning signals, but also for many other reasons such as evaluating model behaviors, augmenting data for low-resource training, producing contrastive explanation, promoting faithful text generation. The latter focuses

[1]Tutorial materials are available at https://contrastive-nlp-tutorial.github.io/

Proceedings of the 2022 Conference of the North American Chapter of the Association for Computational Linguistics Human Language Technologies: Tutorial Abstracts, pages 39 - 47
July 10-15, 2022 ©2022 Association for Computational Linguistics

on the learning algorithm side: how we can use contrastive learning broadly in different NLP tasks. Here is the outline with an estimated schedule.

Part 1: Foundations of Contrastive Learning (60 min)

- Contrastive Learning Objectives (15 min)
- Contrastive Data Sampling and Augmentation Strategies (15 min)
- Successful Applications (15 min)
- Analysis of Contrastive Learning (15 min)

Part 2: Contrastive Learning for NLP (90 min)

- Contrastive Learning in NLP Tasks (30 min)
- Task-agnostics Representation (15 min)
- Faithful Text Generation (15 min)
- Data-efficient Learning (15 min)
- Interpretability and Explainability (15 min)

Part 3: Lessons Learned, Practical Advice, and Future Directions (30 min)

- Lessons Learned (10 min)
- Practical Advice (10 min)
- Future Directions (10 min)

The following subsections give more details with reference papers for each part.

2.1 Foundations of Contrastive Learning

In the first part, we will provide a brief overview of contrastive learning foundations and introduce the most well-known contrastive learning approaches. We start with different contrastive learning objectives including Contrastive Loss (Chopra et al., 2005), Triplet Loss (Schroff et al., 2015), Lifted Structured Loss (Oh Song et al., 2016), N-pair Loss (Sohn, 2016), Noise Contrastive Estimation (NCE) (Gutmann and Hyvärinen, 2010), InfoNCE (van den Oord et al., 2018), and Soft-Nearest Neighbors Loss (Salakhutdinov and Hinton, 2007; Frosst et al., 2019). We then overview different sampling strategies to create contrastive pairs including debiased constrastive learning (Chuang et al., 2020), hard negative samples (Robinson et al., 2020), supervised contrastive learning (Khosla et al., 2020), and adversarial contrastive learning (Kim et al., 2020). We will also talk about contrastive learning with deep neural networks that have shown great successes in vision and language applications such as word2vec (Mikolov et al., 2013), SimCLR (Chen et al., 2020), SimCSE (Gao et al., 2021b), and CLIP (Radford et al., 2021). We will also discuss work on intriguing analyses of contrastive learning (Tian et al., 2020; Purushwalkam and Gupta, 2020; Xiao et al., 2021).

2.2 Contrastive Learning for NLP

In this part, we will first survey the usage of contrastive learning in different NLP tasks. Later, we will also highlight four characteristics that contrastive learning has demonstrated in addition to the promising performance improvement.

Contrastive learning has shown success in many NLP tasks. We plan cover the following: **Contrastive Data Augmentation for NLP** (Shen et al., 2020; Ye et al., 2021; Qu et al., 2021); **Text Classification** (Fang et al., 2020; Kachuee et al., 2020; Suresh and Ong, 2021; Du et al., 2021; Carlsson et al., 2021; Xiong et al., 2021; Qiu et al., 2021; Xu et al., 2021b; Klein and Nabi, 2021); **Sentence Embeddings** (Kim et al., 2021; Zhang et al., 2021a; Sedghamiz et al., 2021) including Quick-Thought (Logeswaran and Lee, 2018),Sentence-BERT (Reimers and Gurevych, 2019), Info-Sentence BERT (Zhang et al., 2020a), SimCSE (Gao et al., 2021b), DeCLUTR (Giorgi et al., 2020), ConSERT (Yan et al., 2021b), DialogueCSE (Liu et al., 2021a). We will also cover discourse analysis (Iter et al., 2020; Kiyomaru and Kurohashi, 2021); **Information Extraction** (Qin et al., 2020; Chen et al., 2021b; Wang et al., 2021d) **Machine Translation** (Pan et al., 2021; Vamvas and Sennrich, 2021); **Question Answering** (Karpukhin et al., 2020; You et al., 2021; Yang et al., 2021b; Yue et al., 2021); **Summarization** (Duan et al., 2019; Liu and Liu, 2021) including faithfulness (Cao and Wang, 2021), summary evaluation (Wu et al., 2020a), multilingual summarization (Wang et al., 2021a), and dialogue summarization (Liu et al., 2021d); **Text Generation** (Chai et al., 2021; Lee et al., 2021b) including logic-consistent text generation (Shu et al., 2021), paraphrase generation (Yang et al., 2021a), grammatical error correction (Cao et al., 2021), dialogue generation (Cai et al., 2020), x-ray report generation (Liu et al., 2021b; Yan et al., 2021a), data-to-text generation (Uehara et al., 2020); **Few-shot Learning** (Liu et al., 2021c; Zhang et al., 2021c; Wang et al., 2021c; Luo et al., 2021; Das et al., 2021); **Language Model Contrastive Pretraining** (Wu et al., 2020b; Gunel et al., 2020; Clark et al., 2020; Yu et al., 2020; Rethmeier and Augenstein, 2020, 2021; Meng et al., 2021; Li et al., 2021b); **Interpretability and Explainability** (Gardner et al., 2020; Liang et al., 2020; Ross et al., 2020; Chen et al., 2021a; Jacovi et al., 2021); **Commonsense Knowledge and Reasoning** (Klein and Nabi, 2020; Paranjape et al., 2021; Li et al., 2021a); **Vision-and-Language** (Zhang et al., 2020b; Li et al., 2020; Dharur et al., 2020; Cui et al., 2020; Radford et al., 2021; Xu et al., 2021a; Jia et al., 2021; Lee et al., 2021a). We will also briefly talk about other applications such as distillation and model compression (Sun et al., 2020), debiasing (Cheng et al., 2021), fact verification (Schuster et al., 2021), short text clustering (Zhang et al., 2021b), out-of-domain detection (Zeng et al., 2021; Zhou and Chen, 2021), robustness (Ma et al., 2021), code representation learning (Jain et al., 2020), active learning (Margatina et al., 2021), knowledge representation learning (Ouyang et al., 2021), adversarial learning (Rim et al., 2021).

In addition to the performance benefit, we highlight that contrastive learning is particularly interesting for NLP because it offers four advantages:

Task-agnostic Sentence Representation As a representation learning approach, contrastive learning has demonstrated its effectiveness to learn task-agnostic sentence embeddings that can be applied across different tasks. Such progress enables efficient encoding of sentences to support large-scale semantic similarity comparison, clustering, and information retrieval via semantic search. The most successful framework is Sentence-BERT (Reimers and Gurevych, 2019) that uses siamese networks with triplet loss to learn sentence embeddings based on cosine similarity. Another example is CERT (Fang et al., 2020) that employs contrastive self-supervised learning at the sentence level with back-translation data augmentation. It outperforms BERT on 7 out of 11 natural language understanding tasks on the GLUE benchmark. Later, SimCSE (Gao et al., 2021b) uses both unsupervised denoising objective and supervised natural language inference signals to learn sentence embeddings. It achieves substantial improvements on several standard semantic textual similarity benchmarks.

Faithful and Factual Consistent Text Generation Contrastive learning is also used to improve faithfulness and factuality of data-to-text generation and abstractive summarization, which has been shown a very challenging issue with the pretrained language models that often hallucinate (Kryscinski et al., 2019; Parikh et al., 2020; Maynez et al., 2020). Shu et al. (2021) propose to improve logic-to-text generation models by designing rule-based data augmentation to create contrastive examples to cover variations of logic forms paired with diverse natural language expressions to improve the generalizability. CLIFF (Cao and Wang, 2021) propose to improve faithful and factual consistency for abstractive summarization by contrasting reference summaries as positive training data and automatically generated erroneous summaries as negative training data. Wu et al. (2020a) also propose to use contrastive learning for unsupervised reference-free summary quality evaluation.

Data-efficient Learning Another advantage of contrastive learning is to facilitate data-efficient learning when training data is not abundantly available such as in zero-shot and few-shot settings. CoDA (Qu et al., 2021) is a data augmentation framework that synthesizes contrast-enhanced and diverse examples by integrating multiple transformations over text. CLESS (Rethmeier and Augenstein, 2020) analyze data-efficient pretraining via contrastive self-supervision through pretraining data efficiency, zero to few-shot label efficiency, and long-tail generalization. CONTaiNER (Das et al., 2021) improves few-shot named entity recognition by performing contrastive learning over Gaussian distributions of token embeddings. VideoCLIP (Xu et al., 2021a) uses contrastive pretraining for zero-shot video-text understanding.

Interpretability and Explainability Contrastive learning provides a new way for promoting model interpretability and explainability. Contrast Sets (Gardner et al., 2020) evaluate local decision boundaries of models by manually perturbing the test instances in small but meaningful ways. Jacovi et al. (2021) propose to produce contrastive explanations for classification models by modifying model representation and model behavior based on contrastive reasoning. Paranjape et al. (2021) leverage prompt engineering over pretrained language models to create contrastive explanations for commonsense reasoning tasks.

2.3 Lessons Learned, Practical Advice, and Future Directions

In this part, we will summarize our discussions of existing work with lessons learned and practical advice. We will also envision the future directions of contrastive learning for NLP such as data augmentation quality and efficiency (Wang et al., 2021b), hard negative examples (Zhang and Stratos, 2021), under-explored NLP applications (Li et al., 2021b), large batch size (Gao et al., 2021a).

3 Reading List

We compile the a light reading list for the audience learning before coming to the tutorial:

- SimCLR (Chen et al., 2020)
- CLIP (Radford et al., 2021)
- SimCSE (Gao et al., 2021b)
- Contrast Sets (Gardner et al., 2020)

4 Diversity

Our presenters come from 3 institutions based in the U.S. and China including 3 male and 1 female researchers on different levels of academic seniority. As contrastive learning can be applied broadly, our tutorial spans many different NLP tasks and domains covering Text Classification and Sentence Embeddings, Information Extraction, Machine Translation, Question Answering, Summarization, Text Generation, Few-shot Learning, Interpretability and Explainability, Commonsense Knowledge and Reasoning, Vision-and-Language, Distillation and Model Compression. Therefore, the audience will come from diverse backgrounds.

5 Presenters

Rui Zhang is an Assistant Professor in the Computer Science and Engineering Department of Penn State University and a co-director of the PSU NLP Lab. He is one of the recipients of 2020 Amazon Research Awards. He serves as an Area Chair at NAACL 2021, EMNLP 2021, and NLPCC 2021. He co-organizes the Interactive and Executable Semantic Parsing workshop at EMNLP 2020 which attracted an international audience with 100+ researchers from diverse academic and demographic backgrounds. He has been working on contrastive learning for few-shot named entity recognition (Das et al., 2021) and text generation (Shu et al., 2021). `https://ryanzhumich.github.io/`

Yangfeng Ji is the William Wulf Assistant Professor in the Department of Computer Science at the University of Virginia, where he leads the Natural Language Processing group. His research interests include building machine learning models for text understanding and generation. His work on entity-driven story generation won an Outstanding Paper Award at NAACL 2018. He is a co-author of an EMNLP 2020 tutorial on The Amazing World of Neural Language Generation. `https://yangfengji.net/`

Yue Zhang is an Associate Professor at Westlake University. His research interests include NLP and its underlying machine learning algorithms and downstream applications. He was the area chairs of ACL (2017/18/19/20/21), COLING (2014/18), NAACL (2015/19/21), EMNLP (2015/17/19/20), EACL (2021) and IJCAI (2021). He won the best paper awards of IALP (2017), COLING (2018) and best paper honorable mention of SemEval (2020). He is the author of EMNLP 2018 tutorial on Joint models for NLP. `https://frcchang.github.io/`

Rebecca J. Passonneau is a Professor in the Computer Science and Engineering Department of Penn State University and a co-director of the PSU NLP Lab. Her area of research is natural language processing, with a focus on semantics and pragmatics. Her work is reported in over 130 journal and refereed conference publications. She won a Best Paper Runner Up at NAACL 2010. She is a tutorial co-chair for NAACL 2018. `https://sites.psu.edu/becky/`

6 Ethics Statement

As contrastive learning often involves data augmentation and manipulation, our ethical consideration mainly focuses on properly dealing with bias in the dataset. As bias and fairness created by contrastive learning algorithms are still under-explored, we will also discuss such relevant topics in the section on future directions.

References

Hengyi Cai, Hongshen Chen, Yonghao Song, Zhuoye Ding, Yongjun Bao, Weipeng Yan, and Xiaofang Zhao. 2020. Group-wise contrastive learning for neural dialogue generation. *arXiv preprint arXiv:2009.07543*.

Hannan Cao, Wenmian Yang, and Hwee Tou Ng. 2021. Grammatical error correction with contrastive learning in low error density domains. *arXiv preprint arXiv:2109.01484*.

Shuyang Cao and Lu Wang. 2021. Cliff: Contrastive learning for improving faithfulness and factuality in abstractive summarization. *arXiv preprint arXiv:2109.09209*.

Fredrik Carlsson, Amaru Cuba Gyllensten, Evangelia Gogoulou, Erik Ylipää Hellqvist, and Magnus Sahlgren. 2021. Semantic re-tuning with contrastive tension. In *International Conference on Learning Representations*.

Yekun Chai, Haidong Zhang, Qiyue Yin, and Junge Zhang. 2021. Counter-contrastive learning for language gans. *EMNLP-Findings 2021*.

Qianglong Chen, Feng Ji, Xiangji Zeng, Feng-Lin Li, Ji Zhang, Haiqing Chen, and Yin Zhang. 2021a. Kace: Generating knowledge aware contrastive explanations for natural language inference. In *Proceedings of the 59th Annual Meeting of the Association for Computational Linguistics and the 11th International Joint Conference on Natural Language Processing (Volume 1: Long Papers)*, pages 2516–2527.

Tao Chen, Haizhou Shi, Siliang Tang, Zhigang Chen, Fei Wu, and Yueting Zhuang. 2021b. Cil: Contrastive instance learning framework for distantly supervised relation extraction. *arXiv preprint arXiv:2106.10855*.

Ting Chen, Simon Kornblith, Mohammad Norouzi, and Geoffrey Hinton. 2020. A simple framework for contrastive learning of visual representations. In *International conference on machine learning*, pages 1597–1607. PMLR.

Pengyu Cheng, Weituo Hao, Siyang Yuan, Shijing Si, and Lawrence Carin. 2021. Fairfil: Contrastive neural debiasing method for pretrained text encoders. In *International Conference on Learning Representations*.

Sumit Chopra, Raia Hadsell, and Yann LeCun. 2005. Learning a similarity metric discriminatively, with application to face verification. In *2005 IEEE Computer Society Conference on Computer Vision and Pattern Recognition (CVPR'05)*, volume 1, pages 539–546. IEEE.

Ching-Yao Chuang, Joshua Robinson, Lin Yen-Chen, Antonio Torralba, and Stefanie Jegelka. 2020. Debiased contrastive learning. *arXiv preprint arXiv:2007.00224*.

Kevin Clark, Minh-Thang Luong, Quoc V. Le, and Christopher D. Manning. 2020. Pre-training transformers as energy-based cloze models. *CoRR*.

Wanyun Cui, Guangyu Zheng, and Wei Wang. 2020. Unsupervised natural language inference via decoupled multimodal contrastive learning. *arXiv preprint arXiv:2010.08200*.

Sarkar Snigdha Sarathi Das, Arzoo Katiyar, Rebecca J Passonneau, and Rui Zhang. 2021. Container: Few-shot named entity recognition via contrastive learning. *arXiv preprint arXiv:2109.07589*.

Sameer Dharur, Purva Tendulkar, Dhruv Batra, Devi Parikh, and Ramprasaath R Selvaraju. 2020. Sort-ing vqa models: Contrastive gradient learning for improved consistency. *arXiv preprint arXiv:2010.10038*.

Yangkai Du, Tengfei Ma, Lingfei Wu, Fangli Xu, Xuhong Zhang, and Shouling Ji. 2021. Constructing contrastive samples via summarization for text classification with limited annotations. *arXiv preprint arXiv:2104.05094*.

Xiangyu Duan, Hongfei Yu, Mingming Yin, Min Zhang, Weihua Luo, and Yue Zhang. 2019. Contrastive attention mechanism for abstractive sentence summarization. *CoRR*, abs/1910.13114.

Hongchao Fang, Sicheng Wang, Meng Zhou, Jiayuan Ding, and Pengtao Xie. 2020. Cert: Contrastive self-supervised learning for language understanding. *arXiv preprint arXiv:2005.12766*.

Nicholas Frosst, Nicolas Papernot, and Geoffrey Hinton. 2019. Analyzing and improving representations with the soft nearest neighbor loss. In *Proceedings of the 36th International Conference on Machine Learning*.

Luyu Gao, Yunyi Zhang, Jiawei Han, and Jamie Callan. 2021a. Scaling deep contrastive learning batch size under memory limited setup. In *Proceedings of the 6th Workshop on Representation Learning for NLP (RepL4NLP-2021)*, Online. Association for Computational Linguistics.

Tianyu Gao, Xingcheng Yao, and Danqi Chen. 2021b. Simcse: Simple contrastive learning of sentence embeddings. *arXiv preprint arXiv:2104.08821*.

Matt Gardner, Yoav Artzi, Victoria Basmova, Jonathan Berant, Ben Bogin, Sihao Chen, Pradeep Dasigi, Dheeru Dua, Yanai Elazar, Ananth Gottumukkala, et al. 2020. Evaluating models' local decision boundaries via contrast sets. *arXiv preprint arXiv:2004.02709*.

John M Giorgi, Osvald Nitski, Gary D Bader, and Bo Wang. 2020. Declutr: Deep contrastive learning for unsupervised textual representations. *arXiv preprint arXiv:2006.03659*.

Beliz Gunel, Jingfei Du, Alexis Conneau, and Ves Stoyanov. 2020. Supervised contrastive learning for pre-trained language model fine-tuning. *arXiv preprint arXiv:2011.01403*.

Michael Gutmann and Aapo Hyvärinen. 2010. Noise-contrastive estimation: A new estimation principle for unnormalized statistical models. In *Proceedings of the Thirteenth International Conference on Artificial Intelligence and Statistics*.

Dan Iter, Kelvin Guu, Larry Lansing, and Dan Jurafsky. 2020. Pretraining with contrastive sentence objectives improves discourse performance of language models. *arXiv preprint arXiv:2005.10389*.

Alon Jacovi, Swabha Swayamdipta, Shauli Ravfogel, Yanai Elazar, Yejin Choi, and Yoav Goldberg. 2021. Contrastive explanations for model interpretability. *arXiv preprint arXiv:2103.01378*.

Paras Jain, Ajay Jain, Tianjun Zhang, Pieter Abbeel, Joseph E Gonzalez, and Ion Stoica. 2020. Contrastive code representation learning. *arXiv preprint arXiv:2007.04973*.

Chao Jia, Yinfei Yang, Ye Xia, Yi-Ting Chen, Zarana Parekh, Hieu Pham, Quoc V. Le, Yun-Hsuan Sung, Zhen Li, and Tom Duerig. 2021. Scaling up visual and vision-language representation learning with noisy text supervision. *CoRR*, abs/2102.05918.

Mohammad Kachuee, Hao Yuan, Young-Bum Kim, and Sungjin Lee. 2020. Self-supervised contrastive learning for efficient user satisfaction prediction in conversational agents. *arXiv preprint arXiv:2010.11230*.

Vladimir Karpukhin, Barlas Oğuz, Sewon Min, Patrick Lewis, Ledell Wu, Sergey Edunov, Danqi Chen, and Wen-tau Yih. 2020. Dense passage retrieval for open-domain question answering. *arXiv preprint arXiv:2004.04906*.

Prannay Khosla, Piotr Teterwak, Chen Wang, Aaron Sarna, Yonglong Tian, Phillip Isola, Aaron Maschinot, Ce Liu, and Dilip Krishnan. 2020. Supervised contrastive learning. *Advances in Neural Information Processing Systems*, 33:18661–18673.

Minseon Kim, Jihoon Tack, and Sung Ju Hwang. 2020. Adversarial self-supervised contrastive learning. In *Advances in Neural Information Processing Systems*.

Taeuk Kim, Kang Min Yoo, and Sang-goo Lee. 2021. Self-guided contrastive learning for bert sentence representations. *arXiv preprint arXiv:2106.07345*.

Hirokazu Kiyomaru and Sadao Kurohashi. 2021. Contextualized and generalized sentence representations by contrastive self-supervised learning: A case study on discourse relation analysis. In *Proceedings of the 2021 Conference of the North American Chapter of the Association for Computational Linguistics: Human Language Technologies*, pages 5578–5584.

Tassilo Klein and Moin Nabi. 2020. Contrastive self-supervised learning for commonsense reasoning. *arXiv preprint arXiv:2005.00669*.

Tassilo Klein and Moin Nabi. 2021. Attention-based contrastive learning for winograd schemas. *arXiv preprint arXiv:2109.05108*.

Wojciech Kryscinski, Bryan McCann, Caiming Xiong, and Richard Socher. 2019. Evaluating the factual consistency of abstractive text summarization. *CoRR*, abs/1910.12840.

Hwanhee Lee, Seunghyun Yoon, Franck Dernoncourt, Trung Bui, and Kyomin Jung. 2021a. Umic: An unreferenced metric for image captioning via contrastive learning. *arXiv preprint arXiv:2106.14019*.

Seanie Lee, Dong Bok Lee, and Sung Ju Hwang. 2021b. Contrastive learning with adversarial perturbations for conditional text generation. In *International Conference on Learning Representations*.

Haonan Li, Yeyun Gong, Jian Jiao, Ruofei Zhang, Timothy Baldwin, and Nan Duan. 2021a. Kfcnet: Knowledge filtering and contrastive learning network for generative commonsense reasoning. *arXiv preprint arXiv:2109.06704*.

Shicheng Li, Pengcheng Yang, Fuli Luo, and Jun Xie. 2021b. Multi-granularity contrasting for cross-lingual pre-training. In *Findings of the Association for Computational Linguistics: ACL-IJCNLP 2021*, pages 1708–1717.

Wei Li, Can Gao, Guocheng Niu, Xinyan Xiao, Hao Liu, Jiachen Liu, Hua Wu, and Haifeng Wang. 2020. Unimo: Towards unified-modal understanding and generation via cross-modal contrastive learning. *arXiv preprint arXiv:2012.15409*.

Weixin Liang, James Zou, and Zhou Yu. 2020. Alice: Active learning with contrastive natural language explanations. *arXiv preprint arXiv:2009.10259*.

Che Liu, Rui Wang, Jinghua Liu, Jian Sun, Fei Huang, and Luo Si. 2021a. Dialoguecse: Dialogue-based contrastive learning of sentence embeddings. *arXiv preprint arXiv:2109.12599*.

Fenglin Liu, Changchang Yin, Xian Wu, Shen Ge, Ping Zhang, and Xu Sun. 2021b. Contrastive attention for automatic chest x-ray report generation. *arXiv preprint arXiv:2106.06965*.

Han Liu, Feng Zhang, Xiaotong Zhang, Siyang Zhao, and Xianchao Zhang. 2021c. An explicit-joint and supervised-contrastive learning framework for few-shot intent classification and slot filling. In *EMNLP-Findings 2021*.

Junpeng Liu, Yanyan Zou, Hainan Zhang, Hongshen Chen, Zhuoye Ding, Caixia Yuan, and Xiaojie Wang. 2021d. Topic-aware contrastive learning for abstractive dialogue summarization. *arXiv preprint arXiv:2109.04994*.

Yixin Liu and Pengfei Liu. 2021. Simcls: A simple framework for contrastive learning of abstractive summarization. *arXiv preprint arXiv:2106.01890*.

Lajanugen Logeswaran and Honglak Lee. 2018. An efficient framework for learning sentence representations. *CoRR*, abs/1803.02893.

Ruikun Luo, Guanhuan Huang, and Xiaojun Quan. 2021. Bi-granularity contrastive learning for post-training in few-shot scene. *arXiv preprint arXiv:2106.02327*.

Xiaofei Ma, Cicero Nogueira dos Santos, and Andrew O Arnold. 2021. Contrastive fine-tuning improves robustness for neural rankers. *arXiv preprint arXiv:2105.12932*.

Katerina Margatina, Giorgos Vernikos, Loïc Barrault, and Nikolaos Aletras. 2021. Active learning by acquiring contrastive examples. *arXiv preprint arXiv:2109.03764*.

Joshua Maynez, Shashi Narayan, Bernd Bohnet, and Ryan McDonald. 2020. On faithfulness and factuality in abstractive summarization. In *Proceedings of the 58th Annual Meeting of the Association for Computational Linguistics*, Online. Association for Computational Linguistics.

Yu Meng, Chenyan Xiong, Payal Bajaj, Saurabh Tiwary, Paul Bennett, Jiawei Han, and Xia Song. 2021. COCO-LM: correcting and contrasting text sequences for language model pretraining. *CoRR*, abs/2102.08473.

Tomas Mikolov, Kai Chen, Greg Corrado, and Jeffrey Dean. 2013. Efficient estimation of word representations in vector space. *arXiv preprint arXiv:1301.3781*.

Hyun Oh Song, Yu Xiang, Stefanie Jegelka, and Silvio Savarese. 2016. Deep metric learning via lifted structured feature embedding. In *Proceedings of the IEEE conference on computer vision and pattern recognition*, pages 4004–4012.

Bo Ouyang, Wenbing Huang, Runfa Chen, Zhixing Tan, Yang Liu, Maosong Sun, and Jihong Zhu. 2021. Knowledge representation learning with contrastive completion coding. *EMNLP-Findings 2021*.

Xiao Pan, Mingxuan Wang, Liwei Wu, and Lei Li. 2021. Contrastive learning for many-to-many multilingual neural machine translation. *arXiv preprint arXiv:2105.09501*.

Bhargavi Paranjape, Julian Michael, Marjan Ghazvininejad, Luke Zettlemoyer, and Hannaneh Hajishirzi. 2021. Prompting contrastive explanations for commonsense reasoning tasks. *arXiv preprint arXiv:2106.06823*.

Ankur P. Parikh, Xuezhi Wang, Sebastian Gehrmann, Manaal Faruqui, Bhuwan Dhingra, Diyi Yang, and Dipanjan Das. 2020. Totto: A controlled table-to-text generation dataset. *CoRR*, abs/2004.14373.

Senthil Purushwalkam and Abhinav Gupta. 2020. Demystifying contrastive self-supervised learning: Invariances, augmentations and dataset biases. *arXiv preprint arXiv:2007.13916*.

Yujia Qin, Yankai Lin, Ryuichi Takanobu, Zhiyuan Liu, Peng Li, Heng Ji, Minlie Huang, Maosong Sun, and Jie Zhou. 2020. Erica: improving entity and relation understanding for pre-trained language models via contrastive learning. *arXiv preprint arXiv:2012.15022*.

Yao Qiu, Jinchao Zhang, and Jie Zhou. 2021. Improving gradient-based adversarial training for text classification by contrastive learning and auto-encoder. *arXiv preprint arXiv:2109.06536*.

Yanru Qu, Dinghan Shen, Yelong Shen, Sandra Sajeev, Weizhu Chen, and Jiawei Han. 2021. Co{da}: Contrast-enhanced and diversity-promoting data augmentation for natural language understanding. In *International Conference on Learning Representations*.

Alec Radford, Jong Wook Kim, Chris Hallacy, Aditya Ramesh, Gabriel Goh, Sandhini Agarwal, Girish Sastry, Amanda Askell, Pamela Mishkin, Jack Clark, et al. 2021. Learning transferable visual models from natural language supervision. *arXiv preprint arXiv:2103.00020*.

Nils Reimers and Iryna Gurevych. 2019. Sentence-bert: Sentence embeddings using siamese bert-networks. *arXiv preprint arXiv:1908.10084*.

Nils Rethmeier and Isabelle Augenstein. 2020. Long-tail zero and few-shot learning via contrastive pretraining on and for small data. *CoRR*, abs/2010.01061.

Nils Rethmeier and Isabelle Augenstein. 2021. A primer on contrastive pretraining in language processing: Methods, lessons learned and perspectives. *arXiv preprint arXiv:2102.12982*.

Daniela N Rim, DongNyeong Heo, and Heeyoul Choi. 2021. Adversarial training with contrastive learning in nlp. *arXiv preprint arXiv:2109.09075*.

Joshua Robinson, Ching-Yao Chuang, Suvrit Sra, and Stefanie Jegelka. 2020. Contrastive learning with hard negative samples. *arXiv preprint arXiv:2010.04592*.

Alexis Ross, Ana Marasović, and Matthew E Peters. 2020. Explaining nlp models via minimal contrastive editing (mice). *arXiv preprint arXiv:2012.13985*.

Ruslan Salakhutdinov and Geoff Hinton. 2007. Learning a nonlinear embedding by preserving class neighbourhood structure. In *Proceedings of the Eleventh International Conference on Artificial Intelligence and Statistics*.

Florian Schroff, Dmitry Kalenichenko, and James Philbin. 2015. Facenet: A unified embedding for face recognition and clustering. In *Proceedings of the IEEE conference on computer vision and pattern recognition*, pages 815–823.

Tal Schuster, Adam Fisch, and Regina Barzilay. 2021. Get your vitamin c! robust fact verification with contrastive evidence. *arXiv preprint arXiv:2103.08541*.

Hooman Sedghamiz, Shivam Raval, Enrico Santus, Tuka Alhanai, and Mohammad Ghassemi. 2021. Supcl-seq: Supervised contrastive learning for downstream optimized sequence representations. *arXiv preprint arXiv:2109.07424*.

Dinghan Shen, Mingzhi Zheng, Yelong Shen, Yanru Qu, and Weizhu Chen. 2020. A simple but tough-to-beat data augmentation approach for natural language understanding and generation. *arXiv preprint arXiv:2009.13818*.

Chang Shu, Yusen Zhang, Xiangyu Dong, Peng Shi, Tao Yu, and Rui Zhang. 2021. Logic-consistency text generation from semantic parses. *arXiv preprint arXiv:2108.00577*.

Kihyuk Sohn. 2016. Improved deep metric learning with multi-class n-pair loss objective. In *Advances in neural information processing systems*, pages 1857–1865.

Siqi Sun, Zhe Gan, Yu Cheng, Yuwei Fang, Shuohang Wang, and Jingjing Liu. 2020. Contrastive distillation on intermediate representations for language model compression. *arXiv preprint arXiv:2009.14167*.

Varsha Suresh and Desmond C Ong. 2021. Not all negatives are equal: Label-aware contrastive loss for fine-grained text classification. *arXiv preprint arXiv:2109.05427*.

Yonglong Tian, Chen Sun, Ben Poole, Dilip Krishnan, Cordelia Schmid, and Phillip Isola. 2020. What makes for good views for contrastive learning? *arXiv preprint arXiv:2005.10243*.

Yui Uehara, Tatsuya Ishigaki, Kasumi Aoki, Hiroshi Noji, Keiichi Goshima, Ichiro Kobayashi, Hiroya Takamura, and Yusuke Miyao. 2020. Learning with contrastive examples for data-to-text generation. In *Proceedings of the 28th International Conference on Computational Linguistics*.

Jannis Vamvas and Rico Sennrich. 2021. Contrastive conditioning for assessing disambiguation in mt: A case study of distilled bias. In *EMNLP 2021*.

Aäron van den Oord, Yazhe Li, and Oriol Vinyals. 2018. Representation learning with contrastive predictive coding. *arXiv preprint arXiv:1807.03748*.

Danqing Wang, Jiaze Chen, Hao Zhou, Xipeng Qiu, and Lei Li. 2021a. Contrastive aligned joint learning for multilingual summarization. In *Findings of the Association for Computational Linguistics: ACL-IJCNLP 2021*, pages 2739–2750.

Dong Wang, Ning Ding, Piji Li, and Hai-Tao Zheng. 2021b. Cline: Contrastive learning with semantic negative examples for natural language understanding. *arXiv preprint arXiv:2107.00440*.

Liwen Wang, Xuefeng Li, Jiachi Liu, Keqing He, Yuanmeng Yan, and Weiran Xu. 2021c. Bridge to target domain by prototypical contrastive learning and label confusion: Re-explore zero-shot learning for slot filling. *arXiv preprint arXiv:2110.03572*.

Ziqi Wang, Xiaozhi Wang, Xu Han, Yankai Lin, Lei Hou, Zhiyuan Liu, Peng Li, Juanzi Li, and Jie Zhou. 2021d. Cleve: Contrastive pre-training for event extraction. *arXiv preprint arXiv:2105.14485*.

Hanlu Wu, Tengfei Ma, Lingfei Wu, Tariro Manyumwa, and Shouling Ji. 2020a. Unsupervised reference-free summary quality evaluation via contrastive learning. *arXiv preprint arXiv:2010.01781*.

Zhuofeng Wu, Sinong Wang, Jiatao Gu, Madian Khabsa, Fei Sun, and Hao Ma. 2020b. CLEAR: contrastive learning for sentence representation. *CoRR*, abs/2012.15466.

Tete Xiao, Xiaolong Wang, Alexei A Efros, and Trevor Darrell. 2021. What should not be contrastive in contrastive learning. In *International Conference on Learning Representations*.

Lee Xiong, Chenyan Xiong, Ye Li, Kwok-Fung Tang, Jialin Liu, Paul N. Bennett, Junaid Ahmed, and Arnold Overwijk. 2021. Approximate nearest neighbor negative contrastive learning for dense text retrieval. In *International Conference on Learning Representations*.

Hu Xu, Gargi Ghosh, Po-Yao Huang, Dmytro Okhonko, Armen Aghajanyan, and Florian Metze Luke Zettlemoyer Christoph Feichtenhofer. 2021a. Videoclip: Contrastive pre-training for zero-shot video-text understanding. *arXiv preprint arXiv:2109.14084*.

Peng Xu, Xinchi Chen, Xiaofei Ma, zhiheng huang, and Bing Xiang. 2021b. Contrastive document representation learning with graph attention networks. *EMNLP-Findings 2021*.

An Yan, Zexue He, Xing Lu, Jiang Du, Eric Chang, Amilcare Gentili, Julian McAuley, and Chun-Nan Hsu. 2021a. Weakly supervised contrastive learning for chest x-ray report generation. *arXiv preprint arXiv:2109.12242*.

Yuanmeng Yan, Rumei Li, Sirui Wang, Fuzheng Zhang, Wei Wu, and Weiran Xu. 2021b. Consert: A contrastive framework for self-supervised sentence representation transfer. *arXiv preprint arXiv:2105.11741*.

Haoran Yang, Wai Lam, and Piji Li. 2021a. Contrastive representation learning for exemplar-guided paraphrase generation. *arXiv preprint arXiv:2109.01484*.

Nan Yang, Furu Wei, Binxing Jiao, Daxing Jiang, and Linjun Yang. 2021b. xmoco: Cross momentum contrastive learning for open-domain question answering. In *Proceedings of the 59th Annual Meeting of the Association for Computational Linguistics and the 11th International Joint Conference on Natural Language Processing (Volume 1: Long Papers)*, pages 6120–6129.

Seonghyeon Ye, Jiseon Kim, and Alice Oh. 2021. Efficient contrastive learning via novel data augmentation and curriculum learning. *arXiv preprint arXiv:2109.05941*.

Chenyu You, Nuo Chen, and Yuexian Zou. 2021. Self-supervised contrastive cross-modality representation learning for spoken question answering. *arXiv preprint arXiv:2109.03381*.

Yue Yu, Simiao Zuo, Haoming Jiang, Wendi Ren, Tuo Zhao, and Chao Zhang. 2020. Fine-tuning pre-trained language model with weak supervision: A contrastive-regularized self-training approach. *arXiv preprint arXiv:2010.07835*.

Zhenrui Yue, Bernhard Kratzwald, and Stefan Feuerriegel. 2021. Contrastive domain adaptation for question answering using limited text corpora. *arXiv preprint arXiv:2108.13854*.

Zhiyuan Zeng, Keqing He, Yuanmeng Yan, Zijun Liu, Yanan Wu, Hong Xu, Huixing Jiang, and Weiran Xu. 2021. Modeling discriminative representations for out-of-domain detection with supervised contrastive learning. *arXiv preprint arXiv:2105.14289*.

Dejiao Zhang, Shang-Wen Li, Wei Xiao, Henghui Zhu, Ramesh Nallapati, Andrew O Arnold, and Bing Xiang. 2021a. Pairwise supervised contrastive learning of sentence representations. *arXiv preprint arXiv:2109.05424*.

Dejiao Zhang, Feng Nan, Xiaokai Wei, Shangwen Li, Henghui Zhu, Kathleen McKeown, Ramesh Nallapati, Andrew Arnold, and Bing Xiang. 2021b. Supporting clustering with contrastive learning. *arXiv preprint arXiv:2103.12953*.

Jianguo Zhang, Trung Bui, Seunghyun Yoon, Xiang Chen, Zhiwei Liu, Congying Xia, Quan Hung Tran, Walter Chang, and Philip Yu. 2021c. Few-shot intent detection via contrastive pre-training and fine-tuning. *arXiv preprint arXiv:2109.06349*.

Wenzheng Zhang and Karl Stratos. 2021. Understanding hard negatives in noise contrastive estimation. *arXiv preprint arXiv:2104.06245*.

Yan Zhang, Ruidan He, Zuozhu Liu, Kwan Hui Lim, and Lidong Bing. 2020a. An unsupervised sentence embedding method bymutual information maximization. *CoRR*, abs/2009.12061.

Zhu Zhang, Zhou Zhao, Zhijie Lin, Xiuqiang He, et al. 2020b. Counterfactual contrastive learning for weakly-supervised vision-language grounding. *Advances in Neural Information Processing Systems*, 33:18123–18134.

Wenxuan Zhou and Muhao Chen. 2021. Contrastive out-of-distribution detection for pretrained transformers. *arXiv preprint arXiv:2104.08812*.

Author Index